MW01065042

LIVING VICTORY

30 DAYS OF VICTORY, BREAKTHROUGH, AND THE FAVOR OF GOD

MICHAEL VIDAURRI, D. MIN.

All Scripture quotations, unless otherwise indicated, are taken from the New King James Version. Copyright © 1979, 1980, 1982 by Thomas Nelson, Inc. Used by permission. All rights reserved.

Other versions used include

AMP—Scripture quotations marked (AMP) are taken from the Amplified Bible. Copyright © 1954, 1958, 1962, 1964, 1965, 1987 by The Lockman Foundation. Used by permission.

ERV—Scripture quotations marked (ERV) are taken from the Easy-to-Read Version. Copyright © 2006 World Bible Translation Center. Used by permission.

GWT—Scripture quotations marked (GWT) are taken from God's Word ®, Copyright © 1995 God's Word to the Nations. Used by permission of Baker Publishing Group.

KJV—Scripture quotations marked (KJV) are taken from the Authorized King James Version. Public domain.

MSG—Scripture quotations marked (MSG) are taken from The Message: The New Testament in Contemporary Language by Eugene H. Peterson. Copyright © 1993 by Eugene H. Peterson. Used by permission.

NCV—Scripture quotations marked (NCV) are taken from the New Century Version®. Copyright © 2005 by Thomas Nelson, Inc. Used by permission. All rights reserved.

NIV—Scripture quotations marked (NIV) are taken from the Holy Bible, New International Version ®. Copyright © 1973, 1978, 1984 by International Bible Society. Used by permission of Zondervan Publishing House. All rights reserved.

NLT—Scripture quotations marked (NLT) are taken from the Holy Bible, New Living Translation, Copyright © 1996. Used by permission of Tyndale House Publishers, Inc. Wheaton, Illinois 60189. All rights reserved.

AUTHOR'S NOTE: Some names of persons mentioned in this book have been changed to protect privacy; any similarity between individuals described in this book to individuals known to readers is purely coincidental.

Copyright © 2014 Michael Vidaurri

All rights reserved

Foreword

"If you found a cure for cancer, wouldn't it be inconceivable to hide it from the rest of mankind? How much more inconceivable to keep silent the cure from the eternal wages of death?" – Dave Davidson.

As an Evangelist I have travelled to the nations of the world preaching the gospel of Jesus Christ because I am convinced it is the only message which brings real transformation and the gift of eternal salvation to everyone who believes (Romans 1:16).

Salvation is a priceless treasure! A gift from God of infinite worth! A miracle without an equal! God's infinite mercy that's too great for words! The gospel has marked a turning point in the lives of countless precious people we have had the honor of presenting it to.

Counseling, psychology, religion, science, education, principles and formulas, all of these things may help with problems and alleviate symptoms; but nothing deals with the root cause of the central problem of humanity like the cross of Jesus Christ. At the Cross, Jesus took our place. He was the substitute for every human being taking the punishment due to us for our sins, upon Himself (1 Peter 2:24).

Jesus' entire mission in coming to this earth was to redeem and restore humanity to right relationship with God. He provided us with all the blessings and benefits available to us as children of God. Because of Jesus finished work on the Cross, every believer has been given a blank check to the bank of heaven and it is our job to cash it in!

Living Victory is a powerful 30 day devotional which explores these truths in wonderful depth and clarity. It will help you gain a greater understanding of how much Jesus has paid for you. God's love for you is not a shallow love, a love that cost Him nothing. No! His love cost Him the suffering and death of His only Son. (John

3:16). God paid this price so we could live a victorious life!

Pastor Mike Vidaurri is a dear friend of our ministry. We studied at Seminary together at Oral Roberts University. I know his heart, and his passion to see believers get ahold of the promises of God, to get ahold of all that Jesus has paid for. As you read this devotional, I want to encourage you to receive by faith, all God has made available for you. I'm excited for you; because of what Jesus has accomplished through the Cross, there is nothing God will not do for you!

Barry Raeburn

Evangelist and Author

www.barryraeburn.org

Introduction

1 Corinthians 15:57 says, "But thanks be to God, who gives us the victory through our Lord Jesus Christ." The Apostle Paul follows this statement with another in 2 Corinthians 2:14 saying, "Now thanks be to God who always leads us in triumph in Christ, and through us diffuses the fragrance of His knowledge in every place." No matter how we describe it, Victory or Triumph, God's will for us is to live BLESSED! To live in the perfect VICTORY that Jesus died on the cross to provide for each of us.

I know what you're thinking and you're right—Jesus never said that we wouldn't face problems, trials, or difficulties, in this life. Difficulties come with the territory of living in the Earth. But Jesus did promise us that through all of the trouble we face because sin exists—we can still have HIS PEACE—WORLD OVERCOMING PEACE! The God kind of Peace, which leads us into VICTORY in EVERY area of life—PRAISE GOD!

You have been given everything you need to succeed in this life, in the person of JESUS. He has given us all things that pertain to life and godliness (2 Peter 1:2). God has provided each of us with THE ANSWER and THE VICTORY over every attempt of the enemy. He has given us the FREE GIFT of SALVATION and GRACE through FAITH in His Son, JESUS! The question I have for you is: "What are you doing with all that you have been given?" Faith in Jesus is the answer that we are all looking for. The moment we take hold of Him and His Word as the FINAL AUTHORITY for our lives, is the moment that we begin experiencing His LIVING VICTORY! Receive all He has for you TODAY. TODAY is the day of SALVATION!

Table of Contents

Day 1
Living Victory

"But thanks be to God, who gives us the victory through our Lord Jesus Christ."

1 Corinthians 15:57 (NKJV)

God has your Victory on His mind. He is believing with you for Victory in every facet of your life and ministry. In fact, YOU are permeating with the smell of Victory over the Curse—permeating with the smell of Jesus! 2 Corinthians 2:14 (AMP) says, "But thanks be to God, Who in Christ always leads us in triumph [as trophies of Christ's victory] and through us spreads and makes evident the *FRAGRANCE* of the knowledge of God everywhere." (Emphasis Added).

Yes, YOU smell—Hallelujah! In fact, you are a beautiful and sweet smelling fragrance to God and to those around you! You even smell good to those who aren't yet saved, because you smell like victory due to your relationship with Jesus. Did you know that your sweet scent is drawing others to you and ultimately to Christ? Even though they may be blind to the truth of the Word, blind to the fact that it is the Lord working in you and through you which is leading you into your victory—they are still drawn to the Blessing of God which is in operation in you because Jesus Christ is in you.

God is so good to His children and the Bible tells us that He is mindful of us. That Hebrew word used in Psalm 8:4 for mindful is the word ZACAR, and it means to be consciously aware of, to take notice of a thing, or to remember it by name. God is so in love with you that He has taken a special interest in all of your affairs. He is watchful and faithful to perform His Word in your life in order to express His great love and commitment to you (See Numbers 23:19, Jeremiah 1:12, and Isaiah 55:11).

There are some who believe that our God is an absent god or a god who doesn't care about His people, but that is the furthest thing from the truth. Our God is an amazing God of Love. In 1 John 4:7-11 (NLT) we learn exactly what our Heavenly Father did to express His love toward us by freeing us from the bondage of sin through the death, burial, and resurrection of Jesus our Savior and Living King.

John writes, "[7] Dear friends, let us continue to love one another, for love comes from God. Anyone who loves is a child of God and knows God. [8] But anyone who does not love does not know God, for God is love. [9] God showed how much he loved us by sending his one and only Son into the world so that we might have eternal life through him. [10] This is real love—not that we loved God, but that he loved us and sent his Son as a sacrifice to take away our sins. [11] Dear friends, since God loved us that much, we surely ought to love each other." God made the provision for our release from slavery to sin through the sacrifice of Jesus—Jesus was in essence our open door to total life victory and freedom.

Paul tells us about the responsibility that God gave to him and to us to proclaim His goodness to all mankind regardless of our opinions about them. Paul says in Colossians 1:26-29 (MSG), "This mystery has been kept in the dark for a long time, but now it's out in the open. God wanted everyone, not just Jews, to know this rich and glorious secret inside and out, regardless of their background, regardless of their religious standing. The mystery in a nutshell is just this: Christ is in you, so therefore you can look forward to sharing in God's glory. It's that simple. That is the substance of our

Message. We preach Christ, warning people not to add to the Message. We teach in a spirit of profound common sense so that we can bring each person to maturity. To be mature is to be basic [or to be singularly focused on the person of Jesus]. Christ! No more, no less. That's what I'm working so hard at day after day, year after year, doing my best with the energy God so generously gives me."

The important thing that each of us need to understand is that Christ can only live inside of us and work through us if we invite Him in. Unlike Satan, Jesus and His Holy Spirit only come in if they are invited in—they do not force their way into our hearts—we must choose to let them in of our own free will. When we do, they will gladly take up residence inside of us and begin to work through us to bring into existence the ZOE life, or the God-kind of life that God predestined for each of us from the beginning.

In John 10:10 Jesus speaks about this ZOE life He came to give us and He contrasts it with the work of Satan when He says, "The thief comes only in order to steal and kill and destroy. I came that they may have and enjoy life, and have it in abundance (to the full, till it overflows)." It is an abundant life that is centered and focused on the person of Jesus which pleases our Heavenly Father. The outflow or the result of that kind of focused life is the Blessing of God manifested in every area of that person's life.

God wants to lavish His love upon His children. He desires to lead them into victory over sin, sickness, and death, but true victory can only come to us when we make Jesus the centerpiece of our lives. When Jesus is at the center—VICTORY, BREAKTHROUGH, and THE FAVOR OF GOD is inevitable. In other words, God will pour out His Blessing on the person who seeks His will and His kingdom over everything else. (See Matthew 6:33). He rewards those who diligently seek Him and obey His commands (See Hebrews 11:6). And part of that Blessing includes giving them a life that they can ENJOY and a life in which He can minister all of His love in abundance, to the full, until it overflows—to them.

That is the kind of life I want to live, how about You? You can if you want to. You can if you'll start by placing Jesus at the center of all you do. You can if you'll dare to Believe His Word (the Bible), and do all that you can to obey and follow Him by making Jesus Lord of your life and being a doer of His Word.

If you're saved, whether you realize it or not—you smell like Jesus! He has put His stamp of approval on your life and sealed you with His Holy Spirit. You have been recreated IN HIM to overcome the Curse and to draw the unsaved people around you—to Him. You don't have to be perfect! You don't have to be a Bible expert! All you have to do is walk in His love, walk in His grace, and disperse your sweet smelling fragrance of God's grace and His love to all of those whom you come into contact.

Paul said it this way in Philippians 2:13-16 (GWT), "[13] It is God who produces in you the desires and actions that please him. [14] Do everything without complaining or arguing. [15] Then you will be blameless and innocent. You will be God's children without any faults among people who are crooked and corrupt. You will shine like stars among them in the world [16] as you hold firmly to the word of life. Then I can brag on the day of Christ that my effort was not wasted and that my work produced results.

Step out in faith today and grab a hold of all that God has to offer YOU—IN CHRIST. Take Jesus and His promises by the hand and begin living the VICTORIOUS LIFE He intended for you. And be that sweet smelling witness of God's Blessing in the earth that draws others to Him. God is Good! Believe it! Receive it! And Live it out in faith today. JESUS IS LORD!

Daily Declaration

Heavenly Father, I willingly give all of myself to Jesus today. I make Him the Lord and Savior of my life. I come boldly to Your Throne of Grace and I ask You to forgive me and to cleanse me of all my sin today! I consciously receive my complete pardon right now, in the name of Jesus. Your Word tells me that when I confess my sins, You are faithful and Just to forgive me of my sins and cleanse me from ALL unrighteousness (See 1 John 1:9).

2 Corinthians 5:17-21 promises me that I have been made the righteousness of God IN CHRIST. I am righteous not because of my works, but because of my faith in Jesus as my personal Lord and Savior. I believe your Word. I receive your forgiveness. And I am determined to begin living the Victorious Life that You have planned for me In Him. Thank You for allowing me to be Your representative in the world. Thank You for allowing me to give off the fragrance of Your goodness to others and to help You in Your work of drawing all humanity to You. I pray all of this in the mighty name of Jesus, Amen.

Day 2
Go Take A Flying Leap…Of Faith!

"Let us draw near with a true heart *in full assurance of faith*, having our hearts sprinkled from an evil conscience and our bodies washed with pure water." (Emphasis Added).

Hebrews 10:22 (NKJV)

Did you know that faith is always spelled R-I-S-K? I am not insinuating that God can't be trusted. Quite the contrary! I am saying that faith always requires us to release our control over our circumstances and to give complete control over to God. I want you to know something that may shock you: *we can either have faith or we can have control—it's our choice*! Faith is relinquishing our confidence in our own abilities, strengths, and influence, and taking hold of God's Word and His ability as Almighty God. Faith rests and relies in God as our *Jehovah Jireh* (The Lord our Provider), in His ability as *Jehovah Rapha* (The Lord our Healer), and in His ability as *Jehovah Tsidkenu* (The Lord our Righteousness). Faith trusts that He will do exactly what He promised us in the Bible. **FAITH IS PUTTING OUR FULL ASSURANCE IN HIM!**

2 Corinthians 5:7 tells us, "For we walk by faith, not by sight." The most difficult aspect of faith for most Believers is continuing to trust God even when things don't look like they are working. We have been trained by experience to make quick counter adjustments, to try to steer ourselves back on course when we lose traction in our faith. But the Bible tells us to rest and trust God even though things may feel foreign to our senses.

The Bible Instructs, "⁵ Lean on, trust in, and be confident in the Lord with all your heart and mind and do not rely on your own insight or understanding. ⁶ In all your ways know, recognize, and acknowledge Him, and He will direct and make straight and plain your paths." (Proverbs 3:5-6, AMP).

Jeremiah 9:23-34 (AMP) says it this way, "²³ Thus says the Lord: Let not the wise and skillful person glory and boast in his wisdom and skill; let not the mighty and powerful person glory and boast in his strength and power; let not the person who is rich [in physical gratification and earthly wealth] glory and boast in his [temporal satisfactions and earthly] riches; ²⁴ But let him who glories glory in this: that he understands and knows Me [personally and practically, directly discerning and recognizing My character], that I am the Lord, Who practices loving-kindness [covenant love], judgment, and righteousness in the earth…"

There is more to this life than what we can understand from our senses. Sometimes the things we are trying to control are really controlling us and interfering with God's Master Plan for our lives. For instance learning to cast our cares upon You. When we hold onto those cares, they consume our thoughts, but when we learn to cast them upon You, we can rest in our faith knowing that You will always cause us to triumph –In Jesus! It is only when we are willing to throw down our staff (our cares and comfort) and trust Him that He can truly take over and deliver us out of the hand of bondage.

In Exodus chapter 4 we see Moses learning this very principle of faith. God called Moses to lead the Hebrews out of captivity in Egypt, but Moses began by giving Him a laundry list of reasons why he couldn't do it—why he wasn't qualified. Then God used an ordinary staff which Moses never left home without, as the instrument to shift his attention from his own power and ability to the power and ability of God. In Exodus 4:2-4 we read, "² And the Lord said to him, 'What is that in your hand?' And he said, A rod. ³ And He said, 'Cast it on the ground.' And he did so and it became a serpent [the symbol of royal and divine power worn on the crown of the Pharaohs]; and Moses fled from before it. [4] And the Lord said to Moses, 'Put forth your hand and take it by the tail.' And he stretched out his hand and caught it, and it became a rod in his hand."

What was God doing here for Moses? He was proving that He can use every day ordinary items and transform them into great instruments that will help us change the world. Moses used his shepherd's staff as a walking stick to get around in the wilderness. He used it as a defensive weapon while tending to his flocks and protecting them from predators. Moses continually had a grip of that staff during the 40 years prior to God manifesting Himself in the burning bush. Nothing miraculous had ever occurred with that staff before. God took what Moses had and transformed it into an instrument that displayed His glory and His power to others. He gave Moses the tools he needed to accomplish His mission for His people. Moses' staff was a symbol that God used to remind him and give him the confidence to believe that God would always be faithful!

For Moses that staff was a symbol of who he was—a shepherd. It was a symbol of his identity and strength. When God commanded him to throw it to the ground, He was saying to Moses, "You're no longer going to be able to trust in your identity, your strength, or your ability alone—you are going to have to shift your confidence and the entirety of your life over into my hands." God was saying the same thing to Moses that He said through his prophet Zechariah, "Not by might nor by power, but by My Spirit, says the LORD of hosts." (Zechariah 4:6).

God is still saying these same words to you and me that He said to these men. He's saying, "Release the control of your life into My hands and watch and see all that I will do with and through you. I will place you before kings, I will use you to deliver and to impact the lives of my people, and I will make your life better than you could ever dream or imagine. But in order for those things to occur, it will require you to take a flying leap of faith, and to relinquish your control over your life by placing it into my hands."

Moses wasn't just throwing down a dumb old stick when he threw it to the ground; he was releasing total control of his life into the hands of Almighty God. He was saying to the Great I AM, "Ok, You are now my physical security, financial security, and relational security. You have become my *El Shaddai*, my All Consuming God!" And like the great hymn written by Judson W. Van DeVenter, Moses was saying to God, "I surrender All."

Let me ask you the same question God asked Moses. What's in your hand? What is it that you are holding onto that has become ingrained in your spirit as your symbol for who you are? What have you allowed to limit your dreams, limit your faith, and limit your momentum? Has it caused you to question your ability in tandem with God's anointing on your life? Is it your bank account? Is it your career? Is it your network of friends? Is it your education? Are you willing to throw down all that you are and to hand **ALL** of the control for your circumstances over to God? Are you ready to take a flying leap of faith and let God be **YOUR** *El Shaddai*, your More Than Enough God? I promise you if you are, it will become one of the most freeing decisions you have ever made!

The first step in taking your flying leap of faith is making this heartfelt declaration of faith: "All to Jesus I surrender, All to Him I freely give; I will ever love and trust Him, In His presence daily live…"

Surrender it all into the hands of God and rest in the full assurance of His covenant love and care for you and all that belongs to you in Him. Our God is a good God. He will never leave you or allow you to fail. Trust Him, and He will lead you into your Promised Land. Dare to take a flying leap of faith—and I promise that you won't ever regret it! If you step out in faith in line with the promises of God—you can rest assured that His Word will **NEVER** return void to Him or to you! His Word will **ALWAYS** accomplish what it was sent out to do. (See Isaiah 55:11).

Daily Declaration

Father, I have decided to cast all fear to the curb and take my flying leap of faith today trusting You with my life. I know that You have Great and Wonderful plans to Bless and to prosper me spirit, soul, and body. I know beyond a shadow of doubt that you love me and have my best interest at heart. I want you to know right now that I believe Your Word and I am confident that You will never fail me. I am stepping out in faith today—laying it all on the line and proving to the world that IN CHRIST, I am more than a conqueror! I gladly surrender all of me in exchange for all of you. Lord Jesus, just like the man in Mark 9:10-25 who brought his son to Jesus for healing, I believe you! I believe that you are able to do the impossible in and through my life. I believe your will for me is wholeness in every area. But just like that man, I ask you to "Help me with my unbelief." To help me remain focused on Your promises when the enemy comes and tries to create doubt with his lies. Help me to stand firm in my faith and planted in You. Today, I declare that just like Moses, I am throwing down my staff. I am drawing a line in the sand and crossing over it once and for all, believing You for complete victory! I call You Lord, I call You Savior, and I call You El Shaddai, my more than enough God, In Jesus' mighty name, Amen!

Day 3
Start Believing For A Little Taste Of Heaven Here On The Earth

"I would have lost heart, unless I had believed that I would see the goodness of the LORD in the land of the living."

Psalm 27:13 (NKJV)

So many Christians spend their entire lives just going through the motions but never really living and enjoying their lives. They act like this earthly life is just something that they must suffer through in order to get to Heaven, where the "real" living will begin. Yes, life will be even sweeter once we are spending it with Jesus, when there is no more pain or suffering. However, if we would dare to believe God's Word and act on His promises, we could experience a little sample of Heaven here in the earth.

Psalm 34:7 declares, "Delight yourself also in the LORD, and He shall give you the desires of your heart." God wants us to enjoy life. He said so in John 10:10 (Amplified Bible) His plan from the beginning was that we would enjoy life and enjoy His goodness just as Adam and Eve did before the fall. They walked with God in the coolness of the day and interacted with Him without limits, receiving all that He had without interruption. But once they sinned—SIN built a barrier between them and the BLESSING OF GOD. Their willful rejection of His commands kept them from receiving all that He wanted to share with them.

When we make God our primary focus He blesses us by giving us the desires of our heart. That is just who He is. Those fulfilled desires add meaning, joy, and thanksgiving for His goodness which is operating in our lives.

In Psalm 52, David contrasts the differences between an evil man who trusts in the fallen World system and the righteous person who trusts in God. "[1] Why do you boast in evil, O mighty man? The goodness of God endures continually. [2] Your tongue devises destruction, like a sharp razor, working deceitfully. [3] You love evil more than good, lying rather than speaking righteousness. Selah. [4] You love all devouring words, you deceitful tongue. [5] God shall likewise destroy you forever; He shall take you away, and pluck you out of your dwelling place, and uproot you from the land of the living. Selah [6] The righteous also shall see and fear, and shall laugh at him, saying, [7] "Here is the man who did not make God his strength, but trusted in the abundance of his riches, and strengthened himself in his wickedness." [8] But I am like a green olive tree in the house of God; I trust in the mercy of God forever and ever. [9] I will praise You forever, because You have done it; and in the presence of Your saints I will wait on Your name, for it is good."

This Psalm is telling us that we need to have hope to propel us forward in this life. We need something and someone to trust in when there is so much negativity and death all around because of sin. David is making the argument here that the "something" we are looking for to give us that hope is the Word of God, and that the "Someone" who establishes that hope is Jesus!

Proverbs 3:5-10 (NLT) declares, "[5] Trust in the LORD with all your heart; do not depend on your own understanding. [6] Seek his will in all you do, and He will show you which path to take. [7] Don't be impressed with your own wisdom. Instead, fear [worshipfully respect and honor] the LORD and turn away from evil. [8] Then you will have healing for your body and strength for your bones. [9] Honor the LORD with your wealth and with the best part of everything you produce. [10] Then He will fill your barns with grain, and your vats will overflow with good wine."

Many of the things that the Bible instructs us to do don't make sense from a rational perspective, but they make perfect sense from God's perspective. And since He knows the end from the beginning and I don't, I'd rather trust in Him instead of my limited knowledge and understanding—how about you?

I know that it can be hard to tithe when there's no food in the house, when the baby needs diapers, or when it looks like you'll run out of money to get back and forth to work if you obey God's command. But when you begin to walk by faith instead of walking by what you understand from your limited knowledge, you are honoring God and making Him your highest priority. As a result of honoring God, He promises us in Hebrews 13:5-6, AMP, "I will not in any way fail you nor give you up nor leave you without support. [I will] not, I will] not, [I will] not in any degree leave you helpless nor forsake nor let [you] down (relax My hold on you)! [Assuredly not!] [6] So we take comfort and are encouraged and confidently and boldly say, The Lord is my Helper; I will not be seized with alarm [I will not fear or dread or be terrified]. What can man do to me?"

In other words, because you have made Your Heavenly Father your highest priority, God makes your priorities His highest priority—He has sworn to Bless and to provide for you with His never ending covenant. When we honor God and His Word, He honors our faith.

The prophet Ezekiel gives us a glimpse of how God looks at covenant relationship in Ezekiel 34:26-27. "[26] I will make them and the places all around My hill a blessing; and I will cause showers to come down in their season; there shall be showers of blessing. [27] Then the trees of the field shall yield their fruit, and the earth shall yield her increase. They shall be safe in their land; and they shall know that I am the LORD, when I have broken the bands of their yoke and delivered them from the hand of those who enslaved them." I want you to know that God always rewards and blesses those who put their trust in Him.

I believe that there are two types of people in this world: the first t is like a thermometer. They only report the conditions that they see and feel around them. When the enemy applies pressure to their lives, these people shift all of their attention and focus all of their energy around all of the negative things happening to them. They walk around sharing their bad report, always talking about how life isn't fair, and asking questions like, "How could God allow this to happen to me?" Yet these people never take any personal responsibility for what is taking place in their lives. Instead they blame everyone else including God for their problems. After they have trampled God's name and reputation through the mud by spewing lies to those around them, they expect God to drop everything and magically solve their problems. I've got news for you; God is not a fairy god-mother nor is He a magician. He is the Creator of the universe who has given each of us all of the tools we need to stop the enemy dead in his tracks and send him scrambling away in fear.

The second type of person is like a thermostat. Instead of giving up, blaming God, or focusing on their negative circumstances, these people see a divine opportunity to use their faith to change their environment. These people know that by focusing on God's Word, His promises for a way of escape, and on the finished work of Jesus on the cross, they will overcome every adversity that the enemy sets before them. These people don't settle for life as it appears, they change it to line up with the Word of God. Instead of whining and speaking about their problems they build themselves up in their most holy faith. They declare the Word of God over their circumstances, and they remind the Devil how BIG their God is.

These people understand that nothing is too hard for God! They speak to the mountains that are standing in their way and command them to be removed and cast into the sea—in the Mighty Name of Jesus. I want you to know every single mountain will obey a person who knows their God-given authority in Jesus, just as He said they would. Mountains have no choice but to move when a Child of God speaks to it in the name of Jesus!

In Psalm 27:13 David shares the passion and conviction of thermostat people when he declares, "I would have lost heart, unless I had believed that I would see the goodness of the LORD in the land of the living." David is being brutally honest and transparent by stating, "I would have fainted, I would have lost all hope, I would have caved in and quit, but there is only ONE THING that changed my entire perspective concerning my "impossible looking" circumstances and kept me moving forward in faith—God's Faithfulness." He learned that he could lean on God who was his Source for provision, for deliverance, and for salvation. David understood that salvation was not limited to being only a ticket into Heaven, at the expense of putting up with the devils junk until he finally made it there. He understood that God did not plan for him or any other Child of God to endure Hell here in the earth—waiting to start enjoying life until we leave this world and enter the next. No! Salvation is wholeness in every area of our lives, spirit, soul, and body, and it begins now in this life!

Quit waiting for heaven to begin living! That isn't God's best! God's best is achieved in us when we recognize who we are in Christ! His best is attained when we arm ourselves with the Word of God—the Bible and our spiritual armor (See Ephesians 6:10-18). And God's best is realized when we become like a thermostat and begin to change our environment with our faith in Jesus, with our confession of His promises, and with the authority of Jesus' name.

When our lives don't match the picture that the Bible tells us we are supposed to be enjoying don't lose heart! Instead, begin to believe to see the goodness of the LORD Jesus here in the land of the living—In The Here And Now—and crank up the heat like a thermostat by declaring God's Word, the name of Jesus, and it will change your environment! God said it! I believe it! And that settles it! AMEN!

Daily Declaration

I declare that no mountain, no problem, no obstacle can stand in my way! I am a child of the Most High God and as such, I have the God-given authority to use my faith and the name of Jesus to change every circumstance that is contrary to God's promises to me in the Bible. I know the will of God for my life because I am a doer of the Word and not a hearer only. I speak Blessing, increase, promotion, divine favor, and perfect health over my body, my family, and over everything that concerns me—in the name of Jesus. The Bible promises me that when I humble myself before God and resist the Devil, he must flee from me. (See James 4:7). Satan, I am serving you notice right now that you have no place and no authority in my life! I am serving you an eviction notice today and demanding that you pack up your junk and get out of my life NOW! I am like a thermostat and I am turning up the heat by speaking only the Word over myself. And I know that positive change is already taking place right now, as I speak. I believe it, I receive it by faith, and I have it right now in the mighty name of Jesus, Amen.

Day 4
Overcoming Temptation

"¹³ For no temptation (no trial regarded as enticing to sin), [no matter how it comes or where it leads] has overtaken you and laid hold on you that is not common to man [that is, no temptation or trial has come to you that is beyond human resistance and that is not adjusted and adapted and belonging to human experience, and such as man can bear]. But God is faithful [to His Word and to His compassionate nature], and He [can be trusted] not to let you be tempted and tried and assayed beyond your ability and strength of resistance and power to endure, but with the temptation He will [always] also provide the way out (the means of escape to a landing place), that you may be capable and strong and powerful to bear up under it patiently."

1 Corinthians 10:13 (AMP)

I get excited reading Scriptures like this. I know what you're probably thinking, *He always says that he loves this Scripture or that Scripture*, but it's true! The Bible is not just a book of rules to follow; it is a book of promises to enjoy and live out—and that is exciting stuff!!!

Look at 1 Corinthians 10:13 (AMP). I like the Amplified Bible because it expands on or amplifies our understanding of the Greek words, and gives us a clearer understanding of what the writers' meant when they were writing to us. Here, the Apostle Paul informs us that no matter what we come up against we have the God-given ability to overcome it, because God Himself is living on the inside of us. It confirms that we aren't unique in our experience concerning trials. The devil uses the same bag of tricks on all of us, trying to move us, or to get us to become emotionally ruled. Finally, this verse tells us that even in our darkest trials, God is a faithful Father who will come to our rescue and lead us in the direction of escape—an escape route which always leads to victory over our adversary—the Devil.

In Matthew 4:1-11 (NKJV), we read about Jesus' temptation in the wilderness after His baptism in the Jordan River by John the Baptist. "Then Jesus was led up by the Spirit into the wilderness to be tempted by the devil. [2] And when He had fasted forty days and forty nights, afterward He was hungry. [3] Now when the tempter came to Him, he said, "If You are the Son of God, command that these stones become bread." [4] But He answered and said, "It is written, 'Man shall not live by bread alone, but by every word that proceeds from the mouth of God.'" [5] Then the devil took Him up into the holy city, set Him on the pinnacle of the temple, [6] and said to Him, "If You are the Son of God, throw Yourself down. For it is written: 'He shall give His angels charge over you,' and, 'In *their* hands they shall bear you up, lest you dash your foot against a stone.'" [7] Jesus said to him, "It is written again, 'You shall not tempt the LORD your God.'" [8] Again, the devil took Him up on an exceedingly high mountain, and showed Him all the kingdoms of the world and their glory. [9] And he said to Him, "All these things I will give You if You will fall down and worship me." [10] Then Jesus said to him, "Away with you, Satan! For it is written, 'You shall worship the LORD your God, and Him only you shall serve.'" [11] Then the devil left Him, and behold, angels came and ministered to Him."

Do you see how Jesus was tempted in these verses? There are three main tactics that the devil uses to get us into sin. In Matthew 4:3 we find Satan saying to Jesus, "[3] *If You are* the Son of God, command that these stones become bread." (Emphasis Added). The Devil always tries to get us to trust in our own abilities instead of depending on God as our Source and Supply. The devil wants us to rely on our hard work, our social influence, and our job and wealth, instead of trusting God and His Word.

at what Jesus says about putting our faith in these sort
thew 6:19-20 states, "[19] "Do not lay up for yourselves
arth, where moth and rust destroy and where thieves
teal; [20] but lay up for yourselves treasures in heaven,
moth nor rust destroys and where thieves do not break
For where your treasure is, there your heart will be

it is that you are trusting in, that is your God. And the
t very clear to us that we can't have two masters.
(AMP) says it this way, "No one can serve two
masters, for either he will hate the one and love the other, or he will
stand by and be devoted to the one and despise and be against the
other. You cannot serve God and mammon (deceitful riches, money,
possessions, or whatever is trusted in [this World's System])."

In Matthew 4:6 Satan again tempts Jesus a second time by
saying, "*If You are* the Son of God, throw Yourself down. For it is
written: 'He shall give His angels charge over you' and, 'In their
hands they shall bear you up, lest you dash your foot against a
stone.'" (Emphasis Added). What is the devil up to here? He is trying
to get Jesus to operate out of pride instead of out of faith. Pride
always says, "Look at me, look what I can do." But faith says, "I
have all the proof I need in the Word of God! Now, watch and see
what my Heavenly Father does because I have believed, acted on His
Word, and trusted in Him."

In John 5:19 we read, "[19] Then Jesus answered and said to them,
"Most assuredly, I say to you, the Son can do nothing of Himself,
but what He sees the Father do; for whatever He does, the Son also
does in like manner."

In John 14:10 we read. "[10] Do you not believe that I am in the
Father, and the Father in Me? The words that I speak to you I do not
speak on My own authority; but the Father who dwells in Me does
the works."

We must understand that *faith doesn't do or say anything that God doesn't do or say first!* Acting on our own without receiving your orders from Heaven first, is in essence, going AWOL. Satan wants you to go AWOL, because doing so will lead you into defeat or get you killed—and make Satan happy because you will no longer be in his way!

Finally, in Matthew 4:8-10 Satan tries to use his third tactic on Jesus, "[8] Again, the devil took Him up on an exceedingly high mountain, and showed Him all the kingdoms of the world and their glory. [9] And he said to Him, *"All these things I will give You if You will fall down and worship me."* [10] Then Jesus said to him, "Away with you, Satan! For it is written, 'You shall worship the LORD your God, and Him only you shall serve." (Emphasis Added).

Here, Satan is playing to both pride and fleshly lusts in exchange for false promotion, increase, and favor—but you and I both know that Satan is a liar, and he never keeps his word about anything!

In John 8:42-44 (NKJV) we read, "[42] Jesus said to them, "If God were your Father, you would love Me, for I proceeded forth and came from God; nor have I come of Myself, but He sent Me. [43] Why do you not understand My speech? Because you are not able to listen to My word. [44] You are of your father the devil, and the desires of your father you want to do. He was a murderer from the beginning, and does not stand in the truth, because *there is no truth in him*. When he speaks a lie, he speaks from his own resources, *for he is a liar and the father of it.*" (Emphasis Added).

Listening, and acting in line with Satan's schemes always leads to death, but operating in line with Jesus always leads to life—The Abundant and Blessed Life!

Now look with me at Ephesians 2:1-3 (NKJV), "And you He made alive, who were dead in trespasses and sins, [2] in which you once walked according to the course of this world, according to the prince of the power of the air [Satan and his way of doing and living], the spirit who now works in the sons of disobedience, [3] among whom also we all once conducted ourselves in the lusts of our flesh, fulfilling the desires of the flesh and of the mind, and were by nature children of wrath, just as the others." What can we learn from this? Paul is saying that before we started following Jesus and imitating Him in both Word and deed, we were doomed to sinful lusts which lead to destruction. Why? Because the Devil never has anything good to offer! All he has are lies, twisted imitations, and promises of things that won't last, because he is doomed because of sin. It may look good for the moment, but the devil is a liar and there is NO TRUTH in him!

I encourage you to take this to heart. When the enemy comes at you like a roaring lion and tries to sway you with temptations, remember that he is a liar! You can't believe a word he says. He may make you an offer that looks good for the moment, but there is always a price to pay for accepting his bribe—and usually the price is your life, your loved ones, your career, your health, or all of the above.

Learn to stop temptation dead in its tracks, send the Devil hightailing it out of your life by reminding him what the Word has to say about him and what the promises of God say about you. Use the name of Jesus, feed on the Bible because faith comes by hearing (See Romans 10:17), and overcome every temptation by standing on the solid foundation which you have In Jesus. Jesus said in John 16:33 (AMP), "I have told you these things, so that in Me you may have [perfect] peace and confidence. In the world you have tribulation and trials and distress and frustration; but be of good cheer [take courage; be confident, certain, undaunted]! For I have overcome the world. [I have deprived it of power to harm you and have conquered it for you.]" Remember this: The Devil is a liar, God is exalted, and Jesus is Lord!!! Amen.

Daily Declaration

I am a fully persuaded that God is for me and that the enemy is defeated! I know that My Lord Jesus has given to me all things that pertain to life and godliness (See 2 Peter 1:2-4), and that in Him I am complete and lacking nothing (See Colossians 2:10). The Bible promises me that God is for me, that the enemy is against me, and that I am triumphant over him because Jesus is my Lord! The Bible is THE TRUTH for my life. I embrace all that the Word of God tells me about who I am. I declare that when I find things in the Bible that I am not obeying at this present time, I will quickly make adjustments in my life to correct those things. Jesus, I give you my life and I ask you for Your help to live my life in a way that pleases you. You said that you came to give me a life that I would enjoy—the abundant and overflowing life—and I am determined to live it out with Your help! (John 10:10, AMP). I declare that I have Victory over every temptation in Jesus, and that when I blow it, I will not beat myself up about it, but I will repent and receive my forgiveness and God's love for me. I pray all of this in Jesus' name, Amen.

Day 5
The Sick Will Be Made Whole

"^{14} Is anyone among you sick? Let him call for the elders of the church, and let them pray over him, anointing him with oil in the name of the Lord. ^{15} And the prayer of faith will save the sick, and the Lord will raise him up. And if he has committed sins, he will be forgiven."

James 5:14-15 (NKJV)

A short time ago I had a friend who called me and asked if I would be willing to meet with one of his friends and pray for her healing. The woman had been diagnosed with stage 4 cancer and was fighting for her life. She was a Christian, but had been, for years, force-fed denominational traditions instead of the Bible. She was raised believing that healing had passed away with the deaths of Jesus and His Twelve Disciples. When we met at her home for prayer, I found out that she had invited some of her close friends to join us. These friends came to give their support and encouragement to their friend even though they did not believe that miracles were still taking place in this day and age.

We need to understand that in order for healings, miracles, and signs and wonders to take place there must be an environment of faith! I felt led by the Holy Spirit to begin my time with this woman and her friends by teaching them about God's desire for wholeness, healing, and total life prosperity in every Christian's life. I wanted this woman to know and to believe that Jesus is the same yesterday, today, and forever (See Hebrews 13:8). If he healed people when He walked the earth 2000 years ago, then He is still willing to heal her, and anyone else who will believe Him today! I wanted to prove to her that no matter how hopeless her situation may have looked, our

God specializes in doing the impossible! Her family, her friends, her loved ones, and even her doctors may have given up on her, but *Jehovah Rapha* (The Lord our Healer), hadn't given up on her!

As I glanced at the faces of the people in the room, there were a lot of frowns and smirks while I was teaching directly from the Bible. These people were supposedly "Christians" who had "supposedly" become saved by believing what the Bible teaches, and by confessing Jesus as their personal Lord and Savior. The problem was that they had obviously spent years building up barriers of unbelief and had become hardened to the truth that God's healing power is still available for all who will believe and receive His promises by faith.

The only two people in the room besides me who looked like they might be receiving what I was teaching, was my friend's son who had come with me to introduce me to this lady, and the woman needing her healing—but that was good enough for me! Yet, my gut instinct was to do the same thing that Jesus did in the home of Jairus the priest, when He went to raise his little girl from the dead. I was tempted to turn over some denominational tables and kick all of the doubters out of the house! Praise God! But even though I knew that would get their attention, it could also cause her to shut down and tune out. I didn't want to risk the only opportunity I had of leading her into believing God's Word and receiving her healing by faith in God and His promises.

In Mark 5:38-43 we read about Jesus and those unbelieving family and friends in Jairus' home, "[38] Then He came to the house of the ruler of the synagogue, and saw a tumult and those who wept and wailed loudly. [39] When He came in, He said to them, "Why make this commotion and weep? The child is not dead, but sleeping." [40] And they ridiculed Him. But when He had put them all outside, He took the father and the mother of the child, and those who were with Him, and entered where the child was lying. [41] Then He took the child by the hand, and said to her, "*Talitha, cumi,*" which is translated, "Little girl, I say to you, arise." [42] Immediately the girl arose and walked, for she was twelve years of age. And they were overcome with great amazement. [43] But He commanded them strictly that no one should know it, and said that something should be given her to eat."

While I was teaching, I told that woman and her friends that in order to receive anything from God they had to have faith! I read Hebrews 11:6 to them which declares, "But without faith it is impossible to please Him, for he who comes to God must believe that He is, and that He is a rewarder of those who diligently seek Him."

I showed them from Deuteronomy 28 that all of the blessings of God belong to those who put their faith and trust in God. I explained from Galatians 3:13-14 and 29, that all of the covenant promises made to Abraham have been transferred to those who have been grafted in by faith in Jesus.

I taught these people that Psalm 103:2-5 promises us that God's desire for all His people is perfect health and wholeness and that these things are included in the benefits which are made available to us as heirs of God's family. This Psalm says, "[2] Bless the LORD, O my soul, and *forget not all His benefits: [3] Who forgives all your iniquities, Who heals all your diseases, [4] Who redeems your life from destruction*, Who crowns you with loving-kindness and tender mercies, [5] *Who satisfies your mouth with good things, so that your youth is renewed like the eagle's*." (Emphasis Added). There are benefits that come with being a Believer In Christ! Praise God!

I showed them that Mark 16:17-18 promised us, "[17] And these signs will follow those who believe: In My name [the name of Jesus], they will cast out demons; they will speak with new tongues; [18] they will take up serpents; and if they drink anything deadly, it will by no means hurt them; *they will lay hands on the sick, and they will recover*." (Emphasis Added). I also taught them that it was not our responsibility to heal this woman—it was God's. But I told them that is was our responsibility to believe that God would heal her based on His Word; that it was our responsibility to speak God's healing promises over her to encourage her faith and ours. And that it was our responsibility to join our faith with hers, according to Matthew 18:18-20, believing for God to eradicate all fear, sickness, and disease from her body.

As I concluded with my teaching of the Bible concerning healing, I told the group that we were getting ready to pray for the woman. I reminded them that we had already proven from Scripture that healing is the will of God for everyone, and therefore we would not be praying, "Lord if it is your will please heal this poor woman…"We had just established that His will is for all of His children to live in PERFECT HEALTH! In fact, Acts 10:38 says of our Heavenly Father, "God anointed Jesus of Nazareth with the Holy Spirit and with power, who went about *doing good and healing all who were oppressed by the devil, for God was with Him.*" Let me ask you something, if healing isn't God's will for mankind then why would He anoint Jesus to heal **ALL** who were oppressed of the Devil? Look what that Scripture says, it says ALL and as far as I know ALL means ALL—not just some of them. Amen!

I then told the group that if they couldn't stir up their faith to agree and believe with us for this woman's complete healing, then it would be better for them to remain sitting quietly off to the side. We didn't want any unbelief to get in the way of our faith or our prayers. I explained to them that we were going to anoint her with oil and lay hands on her according to James 5:14-15 which says, "[14] Is anyone among you sick? Let him call for the elders of the church, and let them pray over him, anointing him with oil in the name of the Lord [Jesus]. [15] And the prayer of faith will save the sick, and the Lord will raise him up. And if he has committed sins, he will be forgiven."

One lady, who had objections throughout the entire time I was teaching, decided not to participate. Even after I read those Scriptures to her straight out of the Bible and even though she could read them with her own eyes, her religiosity still got in the way of her faith and kept her a prisoner to unbelief. She was still adamant that healing had passed away and there was nothing that I could do to convince her otherwise.

I am continually amazed when people can see the truth of the Bible and still reject it because their man-made traditions are more sacred than the words of God.

The good news is that we, Believers, are in good company. We aren't the only ones who had to deal with religious unbelieving people. So did Jesus. In fact, He said of these people, "[6]...You have made the commandment of God of no effect by your tradition. [7] Hypocrites! Well did Isaiah prophesy about you, saying: [8] 'These people draw near to Me with their mouth, and honor Me with their lips, but their heart is far from Me. [9] And in vain they worship Me, teaching as doctrines the commandments of men.'"

Jesus also said in Mark 6:5-6, "[5] Now He could do no mighty work there, except that He laid His hands on a few sick people and healed them. [6] And He marveled because of their unbelief. Then He went about the villages in a circuit, teaching." The implication is that because of the people's lack of faith He could only heal minor things like headaches, fevers, and maybe a runny nose or two. Their lack of faith limited His ability to provide what they really needed and desired. That is just sad.

Finally, looking at the woman who I'd come to minister to, I said, "We have established the truth that it is God's will for you to be healed completely and for this cancer to leave your body forever. We have read in the Bible that, "God has highly exalted Him [Jesus] and given Him the name which is above every name [which is named, including the name cancer], [10] that at the name of Jesus every knee should bow, of those in heaven, and of those on earth, and of those under the earth, [11] and that every tongue should confess that Jesus Christ is Lord, to the glory of God the Father." (Philippians 2:9-11)." I said to her, "Cancer is just a name of a disease that must bow its knee to the name of Jesus!" Then I asked her the most important question of the day, "Do you believe that it is God's will for **YOU TO BE HEALED?**" She answered, "Yes, I believe it is!"

We then prayed for the woman, and commanded the cancer in her body to die and leave, never to return again. (Deuteronomy 28, Psalm 91, Psalm 103, Philippians 2:9-11). I thanked God for the blood of Jesus which frees every Believer from the Curse of sin, sickness, and every symptom of dis-ease in the name of Jesus. (See Galatians 3:29). I spoke healing, wholeness, and complete soundness into every cell, every tissue, and every fiber of her body. (See Isaiah 53:4-5. Matthew 8:17, and 1 Peter 2:24).

I charged her ministering spirits (angels) to go to work for her, protecting her against fear, doubt, and every attack of the enemy that would try to keep her from believing for her complete healing (See Psalm 91:10-13 and Hebrews 1:14). Together we bound all principalities, wicked powers, and demons, that were coming against her and I commanded them to flee in Jesus name (See Matthew 18:18-20 and James 4:7).

Finally, I made a declaration of faith, speaking directly to her spirit, her soul, and her body saying, "In the name of Jesus, I command cancer to be cursed and to leave this woman's body. I command every organ, tissue, cell, and fiber of her being BE HEALED in Jesus name! Body, listen up and obey my words right now—This woman will live a long, healthy, strong, and satisfied life according to Psalm 91:16 which says, "With long life I will satisfy him, and show him My salvation."

I also reminded the Devil about the promise we have in 1 Peter 2:24 (ERV) which says, "Christ carried our sins in his body on the cross. He did this so that we would stop living for sin and live for what is right. *By his wounds you [we] were healed.*" (Emphasis Added).

I told her that if we *were* healed (past tense), then we *are* healed now, and our bodies must line up with that truth in the name of Jesus. After I finished praying for her I told her to call if she needed anything else and left with my friend.

About eight months passed before I heard from this woman again. I ran into her at a gathering but didn't recognize her because she looked so much better. She came up to me and asked if I remembered her. I was a little embarrassed because I knew that I should know who she was, but I didn't. She had a huge smile on her face as she reminded me who she was. She leaned in and gave me a big hug praising Jesus for her clean bill of health.

She told me that the doctors were astonished at her miraculous recovery—they had given up on her and left her to die. Then she thanked me again for taking the time to preach faith into her spirit that evening. She thanked me for the Scripture promises concerning healing that I had left for her that night. She said that she read them over and over and meditated on them every day feeding her spirit with God's promises concerning her healing. She said that it was those Biblical promises that got her through the toughest days during her battle. She admitted that at times it was difficult to believe the Bible over her symptoms, but she was determined to trust God for her complete restoration back to health—just to make the Devil sorry for messing with her! And today, she is cancer-free and a living testimony of God's healing power still at work today in the earth! Hallelujah!

Friends, the Word of God will work every time, if we will just plant it in our hearts and dare to believe God! I encourage you to find a minimum of three Scriptures today that speak to a current situation you are facing. Plant those precious promises in your spirit by meditating on them (Chewing on them, speaking them out of your mouth). Then find someone else who you can encourage with those same Scriptures and share them with them.

We are not alone in our struggles. Your friends, your loved ones, and your co-workers are facing many of the same struggles you are—get out there and minister the Word of Faith to them today.

Romans 10:8-13 says, "[8] But what does it say [The Bible]? "The word is near you, in your mouth and in your heart" (*that is, the word of faith which we preach*): [9] that if you confess with your mouth the Lord Jesus and believe in your heart that God has raised Him from the dead, you will be saved. [10] For with the heart one believes unto righteousness, and with the mouth confession is made unto salvation. [11] For the Scripture says, "Whoever believes on Him will not be put to shame." [12] For there is no distinction between Jew and Greek, for the same Lord over all is rich to all who call upon Him. [13] For "whoever calls on the name of the LORD shall be saved." (Emphasis Added). This isn't just the steps we take to become born-again; these are the steps that we take to receive anything from God: our healing, provision, etc.

I encourage you to tell your friends, neighbors, and co-workers all about God's goodness and faithfulness. If they are struggling with sickness in their bodies, give them a copy of this devotional, write out these Scriptures for them, and then minister the Word of God to them in faith and power!

As you do, you will see God do great and mighty things in your life and in theirs. Stand back and watch as God restores marriages, as He heals the sick and broken hearted, as He delivers them from fear, worry, and shame, and most importantly as He leads them to salvation in Jesus! God's will for all is WHOLENESS, HEALING, NOTHING MISSING and NOTHING BROKEN, in Jesus' mighty name! Amen.

Daily Declaration

I declare that I have VICTORY over sin, sickness, and the Curse in Jesus' name. Lord Your Word confirms to me that You ARE the same YESTERDAY, TODAY, and FOREVER! (See Hebrews 13:8). I believe that since You healed the sick *then*, You are still healing people *today*. I refuse to live by man's traditions! I live only according to the promises from Your Word and my faith in Your faithfulness! Heavenly Father, I declare that You are My refuge and My fortress; My God, and in You alone will I trust." (See Psalm 91:2). You have promised me in Psalm 91-3-16, "³ Surely He [God] shall deliver you from the snare of the fowler [the traps of the Devil] and from the perilous pestilence. ⁴ He shall cover you with His feathers, and under His wings you shall take refuge; His truth shall be your shield and buckler. ⁵ *You shall not be afraid of the terror by night, nor of the arrow that flies by day, ⁶ Nor of the pestilence that walks in darkness, nor of the destruction that lays waste at noonday. ⁷ A thousand may fall at your side, and ten thousand at your right hand; but it shall not come near you.* ⁸ Only with your eyes shall you look, and see the reward of the wicked. ⁹ Because you have made the LORD, who is [your] refuge, even the Most High, your dwelling place, ¹⁰ *No evil shall befall you, nor shall any plague come near your dwelling; ¹¹ For He shall give His angels charge over you, to keep you in all your ways.* ¹² In their hands they shall bear you up, lest you dash your foot against a stone. ¹³ You shall tread upon the lion and the cobra, the young lion and the serpent you shall trample underfoot. ¹⁴ "*Because he has set his love upon Me [as his God], therefore I will deliver him; I will set him on high, because he has known My name. ¹⁵ He shall call upon Me, and I will answer him; I will be with him in trouble; I will deliver him and honor him. ¹⁶ With long life I will satisfy him, and show him My salvation.*" (Emphasis Added). Father, I believe and I receive Your Word as THE TRUTH for my life in Jesus' name, Amen.

Day 6
You're Not Stuck In Your Circumstances—Wake Up Your Soul!

"⁴ I find myself in a pride of lions who are wild for a taste of human flesh; their teeth are lances and arrows, their tongues are sharp daggers. ⁵ Soar high in the skies, O God! Cover the whole earth with your glory! ⁶ They booby-trapped my path; I thought I was dead and done for. They dug a mantrap to catch me, and fell in headlong themselves. ⁷⁻⁸ I'm ready, God, so ready, ready from head to toe, ready to sing, ready to raise a tune: "Wake up, soul!"

Psalm 57:4-8 (MSG)

In Psalm 57and Psalm 142; we find David hiding in a cave from King Saul who is hunting him down in order to kill him. David has become a prisoner to his circumstances. If he comes out of hiding into the open, he will surely be captured and put to death. But if he remains in hiding he is destined to a life filled with isolation, loneliness, and sorrow.

We often face similar fates, feeling as if we are trapped in careers that offer no fulfillment, stuck in bad relationships that offer little to no compassion or love, or overwhelmed and weary by unending debt, sickness, or obligations that leave us with little hope of ever finding true meaning and purpose in our lives.

Just like David declared in Psalm 57:8, it's time to wake up our soul and get ourselves out of the mental, emotional, and even spiritual funk we have allowed ourselves to get into. It's time to begin crying out to God and taking the necessary steps to move towards the change we've desired.

In Psalm 142:1-7 (MSG) David says, "[1-2] I cry out loudly to GOD, loudly I plead with GOD for mercy. I spill out all my complaints before him, and spell out my troubles in detail: [3-7] "As I sink in despair, my spirit ebbing away, you know how I'm feeling, know the danger I'm in, the traps hidden in my path. Look right, look left—there's not a soul who cares what happens! I'm up against it, with no exit—bereft, left alone. I cry out, GOD, call out: 'You're my last chance, my only hope for life!' Oh listen, please listen; I've never been this low. Rescue me from those who are hunting me down; I'm no match for them. Get me out of this dungeon so I can thank you in public. Your people will form a circle around me and you'll bring me showers of blessing!"

David has said in this passage that he has cried out to God spilling out his complaints and spelling out all of his troubles in detail. When we are in the heat of the battle, sometimes all that we can see is the carnage lying at our feet. Our focus has changed from that of proactively taking an offensive approach to life to a defensive approach of just trying to stay alive. When we operate from a defensive stance, we are trying to keep from making waves and being seen by those who are against us. But that is often the type of mentality that keeps us trapped in our personal caves and prisons. We have in essence made ourselves prisoners because we don't want to upset the people around us, or rock the boat by speaking up for what is right. We do this out of fear that if we do, others will care even less for us than they already do.

That is what David was saying in Psalm 57, "There's not a soul who cares what happens! I'm up against it, with no exit—bereft, left alone." If we want to experience real change and come out of our mental, emotional, and spiritual caves once and for all, we must be willing to change our thinking. We must go against the traditional tide and begin crying out to God. Crying out is accomplished by magnifying our BIG God and His UNLIMITED power, instead of magnifying our problems. We learn to steer clear of all complaining and bitterness by focusing on His goodness and unfailing love for us.

Mark 10:46-52 (NLT) describes a similar experience of a blind beggar named Bartimaeus. "[46] Then they reached Jericho, and as Jesus and his disciples left town, a large crowd followed him. A blind beggar named Bartimaeus (son of Timaeus) was sitting beside the road. [47] When Bartimaeus heard that Jesus of Nazareth was nearby, he began to shout, "Jesus, Son of David, have mercy on me!" [48] "Be quiet!" many of the people yelled at him. But he only shouted louder, "Son of David, have mercy on me!" [49] When Jesus heard him, he stopped and said, "Tell him to come here." So they called the blind man "Cheer up," they said, "Come on, he's calling you!" [50] Bartimaeus threw aside his coat, jumped up, and came to Jesus. [51] "What do you want me to do for you?" Jesus asked. "My rabbi," the blind man said, "I want to see!" [52] And Jesus said to him, "Go, for your faith has healed you." Instantly the man could see, and he followed Jesus down the road."

Bartimaeus had been trapped in the darkness and loneliness of blindness. Blindness was the prison and dark cave that he experienced every day. Not only did he live as a prisoner to his blindness, but *his cave* was pitch black and without any beauty. *His cave* was cold and numbing, because of the rejection he faced every day from others. His prison kept him trapped in the belief that he would have to live in his condition forever. We've got to remember that this man had been blind from his birth and there was no known cure for his condition. But instead of focusing on what he did not have, instead of focusing on his troubles and complaining about all of the ridicule and disrespect that he was made to endure as a blind beggar, he focused his attention on the solution that came walking and preaching his way. He focused on his opportunity for change and he began to cry out to Jesus for his healing.

We've got to remember that when we get tired of our present circumstances and begin crying out for change, many people will be quick to tell us to shut up and quiet down. They don't want us to rock the proverbial boat of the status quo. They don't want us to begin moving toward our breakthrough, when they are content to remain the same. They're afraid that if we receive what we're believing for, they'll no longer have anyone to listen to them complain about how unfair their life is. These people become so jealous and put off by our audacity to believe God and to speak up, that some will even become belligerent.

But look at what Bartimaeus did. He moved beyond his soulish limitations and began operating in the Spirit of Faith. He no longer directed the blame for his condition towards the people around him and their lack of compassion. He no longer made excuses about his circumstances but instead, he dared to shout out all the louder even though he knew it would cause others to resent and ridicule him.

In fact, Jesus didn't answer him the first time he cried out. I don't believe it was because Jesus didn't hear him, but because Jesus wanted to see how hard Bartimaeus would fight for what he wanted. He wanted to see how determined Bartimaeus would be to go after what he said he desired or if he'd *cave in* to the opposition and stop short of receiving his sight. Where are you in this process? Are you *caving in* to the opposition you are facing? Or are you willing to fight to receive all that God has waiting for you?

Look what happened to Bartimaeus. Because he refused to cave in to pressure, verses 49-52 tell us that when Jesus called him forward and asked him what he wanted, Bartimaeus didn't hesitate— "I want my sight Jesus!" As a result of his confidence and faith in Him, Jesus said, "Go, for your faith has healed you."

Notice Jesus didn't say, "Let me think about it for a while and I'll get back to you Bartimaeus." He didn't say, "I guess I'll heal you because I feel sorry for you." Jesus didn't even say, "Ok, I've done what you've requested." No! Jesus said, *"Your faith has healed you!"* (Emphasis Added).

In other words, Jesus said now that you have thrown off the restraints or the garment of depression, blame, and excuses which once identified you as being a prisoner to your circumstances and confined to your cave, you've been set-free by YOUR FAITH! It is by YOUR FAITH that you have been loosed from those oppressive circumstances and limitations that in the past kept you bound.

I dare you to be as bold as Bartimaeus, or to do as David did in Psalm 57, and decide to give yourself an emotional, mental, and spiritual wake up call. Don't allow negative thinking, fears of what others might think of you, or misguided perceptions of God's character, stop you from escaping your own prison or from reaching your dreams.

Instead, stand up straight and embrace the boldness that comes from knowing the Word of God and knowing who you are IN CHRIST JESUS! Resist the fear to quiet down just because others aren't willing to speak up for themselves. Believe your way to wholeness, to complete victory in Jesus, whatever breakthrough you need to manifest in your life. God is for you! He is waiting for you to cry out to Him. And, He is willing to call you out of the crowd, out of your cave, out of your personal prison, and into total life fulfillment in Him. You don't have to be trapped any longer by your circumstances—wake up your soul to all of the possibilities of your faith in Jesus!

Daily Declaration

I refuse to remain a prisoner to anything or anyone. Jesus has redeemed me from the curse of the Law, having become a curse for me...that the blessing of Abraham might come upon me in Christ Jesus, that I might receive the promise of the Spirit through faith. (See Galatians 3:13-14). Jesus has freed me from every symptom of the Curse and He has made a promise to me saying, "Therefore if the Son makes you free, you shall be free indeed." (John 8:36). In fact 2 Corinthians 3:17 (AMP) declares to those of us who are in Christ, "Now the Lord is the Spirit, and where the Spirit of the Lord is, there is liberty (emancipation from bondage, freedom)." Hallelujah! I AM free! I AM BLESSED! I AM redeemed by the blood of Jesus! I refuse to live in the bondage of fear, guilt, shame, or under the pressures of trying to please anyone other than My God who is madly in love with me. This doesn't mean that I will be rude or unkind, because I live and operate in the spirit of love. But it does mean that I will no longer be afraid to stand up for what rightfully belongs to me as a joint-heir with Jesus. It means that I won't allow people, or the Devil, to silence me and keep me from crying out to My Lord. I am no longer a person who is limited by trying to please people, but I AM determined to live my life in a way that is pleasing to God. My circumstances will not limit me! They will not keep me bound or hiding as a prisoner to fear! I declare and receive my freedom in Jesus this day, in Jesus' name, Amen.

Day 7
Finding Your Identity In Christ

"⁸ Then he said to his servants, 'The wedding is ready, but those who were invited were not worthy. ⁹ Therefore go into the highways, and as many as you find, invite to the wedding.' ¹⁰ So those servants went out into the highways and gathered together all whom they found, both good and bad. And the wedding hall was filled with guests. ¹¹ "But when the king came in to see the guests, he saw a man there who did not have on a wedding garment. ¹² So he said to him, 'Friend, how did you come in here without a wedding garment?' And he was speechless. ¹³ Then the king said to the servants, 'Bind him hand and foot, take him away, and cast him into outer darkness; there will be weeping and gnashing of teeth.' ¹⁴ "For many are called, but few are chosen."

Matthew 22:8-14 (NKJV)

I was a little confused the first few times I read this parable. In it, the king is hosting a wedding feast for his son. He invites all of his friends and relatives but they all turn down his invitation. The king does not want to waste all that has been prepared, so he sends out his servants to invite anyone who is willing to honor him by receiving his invitation to the festivities. But the confusing part occurs when the king gets mad at one of his guests who is not dressed properly. This guest isn't wearing the proper wedding attire and because of this, the Bible says that this gracious king throws the man into outer darkness and there is weeping and wailing and gnashing of teeth.

I can understand that the king or anyone else for that matter would be upset with someone showing up to a formal event in shorts, a tee shirt, and flip-flop sandals. But why would the generous king, who is a symbol of God, send the man to hell (to outer darkness), when He invited him to the party in the first place? It doesn't seem fair to hold the ignorant, ill-advised, and unsuspecting man, to the same standards that He would a more sophisticated or educated person who has been taught proper etiquette or protocol for wedding ceremonies?

To my amazement however, I learned that the Jews who heard Jesus teach this parable understood His message perfectly. In their society it was customary for everyone who was invited to such gatherings to receive a "Wedding Garment" which had traditionally been emblazoned with the king's coat of arms. This symbol illustrated that those in attendance, those who were wearing the king's emblem identified with, or were subject to, the king's authority. The man in the parable was a traitor. He was a wolf in sheep's clothing. He had been invited to the wedding banquet but he refused to give reasonable honor or respect to the king for his immeasurable grace and charity. In a sense, this man was spitting in the king's face and making a mockery of him and the wedding party. He was blatantly being defiant and refusing to submit to the king's authority.

Finally, this parable made sense to me. The king wasn't expecting anything that was unreasonable. Everyone knew what was expected of them when they were invited to attend this type of ceremony. Even peasants, the poorest and least educated in the kingdom, understood, and or had the opportunity to learn the proper etiquette because this had been a long-held custom or standard. But this improperly dressed guest was blatantly creating a scene and disrupting the wedding reception with his arrogant, unthankful, you owe it to me, entitlement behavior, and therefore security was called to remove him from the feast.

Do you see how this relates to the Kingdom of Heaven? If you and I have not identified ourselves with Jesus and come under His authority as our Lord and Savior, we are not welcome to the Lord's banquet for the Bride of Christ—The Church. Receiving Jesus as the Lord of our lives is the prerequisite, the ticket to ride, or the door opener, to all of the Blessing of God. Without His emblem—The seal of the Holy Spirit—we are foreigners to the commonwealth of His grace and love.

Ephesians 1:12-14 says it this way, "[12] That we who first trusted in Christ should be to the praise of His glory. [13] In Him you also trusted, after you heard the word of truth, the gospel of your salvation; in whom also, having believed, *you were sealed with the Holy Spirit of promise, [14] who is the guarantee of our inheritance* until the redemption of the purchased possession, to the praise of His glory." (Emphasis Added). After we identify with Jesus through receiving Him as Lord, we immediately become Heirs to the Promises of the Bible—we become sons and daughters of the Most High King.

Ephesians 2:11-13 clarifies this even more, "[11] Therefore remember that you, once Gentiles in the flesh [outsiders or foreigners to the King's table] who are called Uncircumcision by what is called the Circumcision made in the flesh by hands [12] that at that time you were without Christ, being aliens from the commonwealth of Israel and strangers from the covenants of promise, having no hope and without God in the world. [13] But now in Christ Jesus you who once were far off have been brought near by the blood of Christ."

I love that word commonwealth; it is a compound of two words: common and wealth. God is not opposed to sharing **ALL** that He has with His children, and He is not broke, barely getting by, or in financial turmoil! The word commonwealth also refers to citizenship within a kingdom. As citizens of the Kingdom of Heaven, we have been afforded rights which we can freely take part in. These benefits include His grace, His healing, His righteousness, His sanctification,

His Holy Spirit anointing, and many more benefits.

Paul tells us in Colossians 1:25-28 (ERV) what our identification in Jesus Christ is all about, "[25] I became a servant of the church because God gave me a special work to do. This work helps you. My work is to tell the complete message of God. [26] This message is the secret truth that was hidden since the beginning of time. It was hidden from everyone for ages, but now it has been made known to God's holy people. [27] God decided to let his people know just how rich and glorious that truth is. That secret truth, which is for all people, is that Christ lives in you, his people. He is our hope for glory. [28] So we continue to tell people about Christ. We use all wisdom to counsel every person and teach every person. We are trying to bring everyone before God as people who have grown to be spiritually mature in Christ."

That is what Identification is all about. It is about leaving behind the old, fallen, and sinful man with all of his flaws and shortcomings. It is about ridding ourselves of our identity crisis, and becoming identified with Jesus who is the perfect and complete image of God. This new identity of ours recognizes and receives the finished work of the cross and understands that now that we are IN CHRIST, it is not about what we can do, but what Jesus has already done for us.

Like the Apostle Paul, our identification has become complete IN CHRIST. Knowing this, we can truly say, "I have been crucified with Christ; it is no longer I, who live, but Christ lives in me; and the life which I now live in the flesh I live by faith in the Son of God, who loved me and gave Himself for me." (See Galatians 2:20).

It is through our new understanding of who we are IN CHRIST that we will no longer be cheated out of what He has obtained and made available to us. Colossians 2:8-10 (NLT) confirms that we are complete IN HIM. "[8] Don't let anyone capture you with empty philosophies and high-sounding nonsense that come from human thinking and from the spiritual powers of this world, rather than from Christ. [9] For in Christ lives all the fullness of God in a human body.

MICHAEL VIDAURRI, D. MIN.

[10] So you also are complete through your union with Christ, who is the head over every ruler and authority."

Take the time to find out who you are IN CHRIST JESUS. Begin to embrace your identity IN HIM. I like what Mark Hankins says: "You look better IN CHRIST than you do outside of Him, and you have never looked as good as you do now IN CHRIST."

It's true; you are a whole new species of being once you join God's family. You are More Than A Conqueror IN CHRIST (See Romans 8:37). Be sure that you find your NEW identity IN HIM and then enjoy the KING'S Wedding Banquet called YOUR LIFE IN CHRIST!!!

Daily Declaration

I declare that not only have I put on the Lord Jesus, but I will also put on the garment of praise which is pleasing to my Heavenly Father. Romans 13:14 (AMP) instructs me to clothe myself with the Lord Jesus Christ (the Messiah), and Isaiah 61:3 (NIV) tells me to put on a garment of praise instead of a spirit of despair. I choose to live my life in this manner so that My God receives glory from my life and so that all who come in contact with me will be drawn closer to Him. Just like the Apostle Paul declared, I declare today that, "I am not ashamed of the Gospel (good news) of Christ, for it is God's power working unto salvation [for deliverance from eternal death] to everyone who believes with a personal trust and a confident surrender and firm reliance in Him..." (Romans 1:16, AMP). I willfully chose Jesus as my Lord and Savior. He is my All-in-All and I AM complete in Him lacking nothing beneficial. (Colossians 2:8-10, Psalm 34:10, and Psalm 84:11). I want the world to know that I AM secure in my identity IN CHRIST! My job doesn't define me. My education does not limit me. My family of origin and all of its flaws and shortcomings will not determine my destiny! I find my true identity IN JESUS and in those precious promises He has made to me in the Bible. I Am who God says I am. I can do everything that God said I can do. And I have **ALL** that God promised that I can have IN HIM! God loves me with an immeasurable never ending love. And IN HIM I live and move and have my being (See Acts 17:28). I pray all of this in Jesus' mighty name, Amen.

Day 8
Do You Have A Merry Heart Or Are You Rotting From Within?

"A merry heart does good, like medicine, but a broken spirit dries the bones."

Proverbs 17:22 (NKJV)

When it comes to life, attitude is everything! If you are always looking at things from a negative perspective then negativity is all you will experience. Those of us who are optimistic may experience setbacks but we won't remain there. Instead, we will move forward into victory and a place of triumph.

The Bible tells us that negativity has the ability to suck the life out of a person, and out of those around them. Proverbs 12:25 says, "Anxiety in the heart of man causes depression, but a good word makes it glad."

Proverbs 15:13-15 tells us, "[13] A merry heart makes a cheerful countenance, but by sorrow of the heart the spirit is broken. [14] The heart of him who has understanding seeks knowledge, but the mouth of fools feeds on foolishness. [15] All the days of the afflicted are evil, but he who is of a merry heart has a continual feast."

When we focus on the good in our lives instead of the negative, our eyes are opened to all of the tremendous Blessings which God has given to us and we recognize that His goodness never ends.

Have you ever heard the phrase, "Don't make a mountain out of a mole hill? Well there is some truth to that statement. Even the smallest inconvenience, the tiniest problem, the minutest detail, can be magnified into something bigger than it really is. This is how worry and fear get their power in our lives.

When we allow these devilish tactics to irritate us, and to fester into something bigger than our knowledge of who God is in our lives—our problems become magnified into huge monstrosities and our fears become elevated towering over our faith in God.

One of the greatest lessons I ever learned was gained while watching a Veggie Tales episode with my kids. In that children's cartoon, I learned something that I had always known, but it took an animated, dancing, and singing asparagus to really drive it home for me. I sat there amazed as Jr. Asparagus sang, *"God is bigger than the Boogie man."* It was then that I learned that fear only had the power that I allowed it to have over my life. If I refused to fear and instead relied on God's Word—Fear had no power. But when I gave in to the Devil's lies, and dwelled on the images that he was trying to plant in my mind, those fears became bigger and began to torment me.

That is why the Apostle Paul instructs us to cast down imaginations and every high thing that exalteth itself against the knowledge of God, and bringing into captivity every thought to the obedience of Christ." (2 Corinthians 10:5, KJV). And also why 1 John 4:18 tells us, "There is no fear in love [in God]; but perfect love casts out fear, because fear involves torment. But he who fears has not been made perfect [or mature] in love [who is God]."

Once we realize this truth, then Scriptures like Isaiah 54:17 really start to revolutionize our lives, "No weapon formed against you shall prosper, and every tongue which rises against you in judgment you shall condemn. This is the heritage of the servants of the LORD, and their righteousness is from Me," says the LORD."

Scriptures like Philippians 4:13 begin to echo God's will for our lives and ignite faith within our spirit man, "I can do all things through Christ who strengthens me."

And finally, Scriptures like Nehemiah 8:10 encourage us to press forward in faith believing that, "The joy of the LORD is our strength." All of these truths begin to change our perceptions about every difficult situation that we face and create within us a merry heart. They create a heart that is filled with the hope and expectation for God's faithfulness to manifest in us, though us, and around us. They create the faith within us to believe that God will rescue us from sin's grasp and lead us into His amazing grace, divine favor, and supernatural Blessing.

God's Word has the ability to change every situation and make it good! We need to understand that it is our job to feed on the Word of God and to change our personal experience by meditating and speaking His promises over our circumstances. When we make His Word our standard for life, we exalt Jesus as OUR SOLUTION to all of life's problems.

Proverbs 3:7-8 commands us, "[7] Do not be wise in your own eyes; fear [reverence, have holy respect for] the LORD and depart from evil. [8] It will be health to your flesh, and strength to your bones."

The Bible says this same thing in Proverbs 4:20-23, "[20] My son, give attention to my words; incline your ear to my sayings. [21] Do not let them depart from [before] your eyes; keep them in the midst of your heart; [22] for they are life to those who find them, and health to all their flesh. [23] Keep your heart with all diligence, for out of it spring the issues of life."

Do your part by driving out every symptom of negativity and fear. Don't allow thoughts of defeat and destruction to cross your mind. Instead renew your mind to the Word of God by meditating on Bible promises day and night. Become a person of the Word. Laugh at the devil every time he comes knocking at the door of your spirit telling you that you can't achieve something. Remember that with

Jesus as YOUR Lord, you can accomplish everything you desire. God told us that a merry heart overcomes every obstacle that is set before it, because a merry heart is a heart that is filled with faith knowing that, "If God is for us, who can be against us?" (See Romans 8:31).

Daily Declaration

I declare that I have a merry heart which is steadfast and secure in my Lord Jesus Christ. I receive every good thing that God has for me through my faith and understanding of His Word. God is for me! He loves me! And has seated me in a place of authority with Jesus! In fact Ephesians 2:4-9 tells me, "[4] But God, who is rich in mercy, because of His great love with which He loved me, [5] even when I was dead in trespasses, made me alive together with Christ (by grace I have been saved), [6] and raised me up together, and made me to sit together in the heavenly places in Christ Jesus, [7] that in the ages to come He might show the exceeding riches of His grace in His kindness toward me in Christ Jesus. [8] For by grace I have been saved through faith, and that not of myself; it is the gift of God, [9] not of works, lest I should boast." (Personalized for more emphasis).

I am whole in Jesus and I am maturing day by day in Him. Holy Spirit, I ask you to lead and to guide me into all truth. Open the eyes of my understanding so that I will know what is the hope of His calling, what are the riches of the glory of His inheritance in the saints, [19] and what is the exceeding greatness of His power toward me because I believe, according to the working of His mighty power [20] which He worked in Christ when He raised Him from the dead and seated Him at His right hand in the heavenly places, [21] far above all principality and power and might and dominion, and every name that is named, not only in this age but also in that which is to come." (See Ephesians 1:18-21, personalized for more emphasis). I pray all of these things in Jesus' name, Amen.

Day 9
Should I Stay Or Should I Go:
Learning To Trust God

"Now the LORD had said to Abram: "Get out of your country, from your family and from your father's house, to a land that I will show you. [2] I will make you a great nation; I will bless you and make your name great; and you shall be a blessing. [3] I will bless those who bless you, and I will curse him who curses you; and in you all the families of the earth shall be blessed." [4] So Abram departed as the LORD had spoken to him."

Genesis 12:1-4 (NKJV)

One of the hardest decisions we make is deciding whether or not we will trust and follow God when we can't see our end destination. Fear and anxiety often try to creep in and convince us that if we step out in faith we may fail or make an uncorrectable mistake. Satan works hard at getting us to second guess ourselves and doubt the Word of God. He raises questions in our minds like, "What if what I thought I heard really wasn't God but just me?" Or maybe thoughts like, "What if I step out in faith and fail?"

When fearful thoughts like these come our way, we often overlook the fact that Satan is terrified at the thought of us hearing and obeying the voice of God. He knows that if we become proficient at acting on the Word—his authority in the earth will come to an end. His only recourse is to cause us to fear the "What Ifs" and stay with what's "familiar."

Our courage to venture out into the Arena of Faith is a sure deathblow to his satanic regime. Yet, if he can convince us to become comfortable and fearful of change then he can keep us paralyzed in immobility—through groundless unbelief and fear.

When my wife Patty and I decided to leave California, to attend Oral Robert's University, I was excited to get the heck out of Dodge and start a new chapter in our lives. Yet at the same time, we were leaving all of our family and friends. Patty was pregnant with our second child and only two weeks away from her delivery date. She had decided to stay behind in California temporarily, so that she could keep the same doctor who had delivered our son. She didn't want to try to find a new doctor since she was so close to her delivery date. Both she and my two year old son stayed with her mother in California and I left for School in Oklahoma

I was a bit of a wreck thinking that I might not make it back to California for the birth of our second child. I felt like a traitor! How could I go away and possibly miss such an important life event—the birth of our daughter? Wasn't it more important for me to be with my wife for support than to be two thousand miles away at school? It just didn't seem right! I was sick to my stomach with guilt and thoughts that I was acting selfishly.

Part of my dilemma was due to the fact that I had just quit my career in the Medical/Pharmaceutical industry and all of our finances were currently tied up in renovations we had made to our home. We had recently remodeled the entire house in order to sale it quickly. E renovations had gone over budget and I had no money for my move to Tulsa, Oklahoma.

But wait that wasn't it! The transmission in my newer Mercedes ML320 SUV had just gone out a two days after we sowed our other car to a lady in need. To top that off, the company I had been working for notified me that I would not be receiving the $17,000 bonus check that I had worked so hard to earn, on the grounds that I was leaving before the end of the fiscal year. It was ridiculous! The bonus check was for commissions I had earned from the beginning of the year—work which had already been completed—and had nothing to do with finishing out the year. I was in a huge predicament; I had no clue where I was going to live once I arrived in Tulsa. I had planned on using that bonus to find an apartment, but my school supplies, California just in time for my daughter's birth, but what was I going to do now? Talk about feeling stuck between a rock and a hard place!

I was plagued with thoughts that maybe I had missed God. Maybe I was doing something that really wasn't God's plan—after all, it wasn't going as easily as I thought it should be. If God had really wanted me to go to seminary shouldn't everything have fallen right into place?

I have since learned that it is the stretching of our faith and walking out His plan even when we cannot "see" the light at the end of our tunnel—that makes us truly victorious. It is our becoming fully dependent on Him as our God and Source for all things—which allows Him to do the miraculous in our personal lives. When we trust Him, He opens up the doors to His extraordinary and miraculous provision! That is exactly what happened with Abraham and every other FAITH GIANT we read about in Hebrews chapter 11. They all had to learn to trust God in the midst of the impossible—all the way into their very own Promised Land.

Hebrews 11:8 tells us, "By faith Abraham obeyed when he was called to go out to the place which he would receive as an inheritance. And he went out, not knowing where he was going." This is the reason that so many people fail to realize their dreams. They have become enslaved to the fear of what if… They are too afraid to step out on the ocean of faith and trust God because of their fear of sinking and drowning. It is much easier to remain in the boat where everything is dry and comfortable than it is to kick our legs over the side and walk on the water toward Jesus. But faith is always the prerequisite for the miraculous.

Hebrews 11:6 (GWT) tells us, "No one can please God without faith. Whoever goes to God must believe that God exists and that he rewards those who seek him."

God's provision for all of my needs began to manifest the day before I left for ORU. It all started with my next door neighbor, who thought I had lost my marbles. For years our families had attended the same Baptist Church. We'd served together, and had taken just about every Bible study class they offered. Two years prior however, we had left that church to attend a non-denominational Charismatic church that we really enjoyed. When I told my friend that Patty and I had decided to move to Tulsa to attend ORU, he began to warn me about the so called scandals that had occurred during the 1960's concerning Oral Roberts and his pleas for help while building the City of Faith (a medical hospital that merged medicine with prayer). I assured him that I had heard the rumors and was not moved by those accusations and allegations.

The day before I left for Tulsa, my neighbor walked over to my house (probably to his own amazement), and handed me a check for $800.00, saying, "I don't know exactly why I am doing this. I think you are making a huge mistake, but here you go. Jan and I wanted to give you a going away gift and let you know that we love you."

That same day, a lady from our church came over and gave me a check for $1000.00. She said that God had told her that I needed that money and she was the one who was supposed to give it to me. Combined, those two checks were enough to pay for one month's COBRA insurance for the delivery of my daughter, and for food and lodging on my trip to Oklahoma.

My mother also called and asked if I would allow her to come along as company during the trip. She agreed to help pay for the gas, lodging, and food and she even agreed to help with the driving—this was yet another blessing and provision of God!

I have learned that it's not out of the ordinary for God to show up at 11:59, when you need to have the answer to your miracle by 12:00. But praise God! He shows up!

The only remaining dilemma was that I still had no idea where I was going to live once I got to Tulsa. I was ready to do whatever was necessary, even if it meant sleeping in my car and taking showers in the gym every morning until I got a job and could afford an apartment.

We arrived in Tulsa on Sunday evening. The only hotel we could find was a Motel 6 in a bad neighborhood. Everyone was in town for the new semester and all of the hotels near the school were booked to capacity with no vacancies. Many of the student's parents had come into town just as my mom had, to see their kids off—the only difference was that I was a 33 year old kid and most of the other students were in their late teens.

That night I couldn't sleep because of the anxiety I was feeling and because of all the gun shots that echoed through the hallways of that Motel 6. I wondered again what I had gotten myself into. My mom would be flying home in a couple of days and then I'd really be on my own.

The next morning at 8 a.m., I walked into orientation, looked over to the right side of the room, and saw two friends I had met during Grad College Weekend (a week long opportunity to visit the school and see what college life at ORU would be like). Elijah and Reggie came over, gave me a hug as if we'd been long time friends. They asked when I had arrived and where I was staying. Not wanting anyone to know my predicament, I explained that I had just arrived the night before and was staying in a Motel 6 across town. Immediately, Elijah slapped me on the back and said, "Man, don't waste your money, come stay with me. I live across the street from the school in a two bedroom apartment. It's just me and my dog and all that room. You can stay as long as you need to, RENT FREE!"

I was amazed! I had only met Elijah during a one week visit to Tulsa to determine if I wanted to attend school at ORU, and he was offering me a place to stay. I immediately accepted his generous offer, but knew that God was behind it all. I was reminded once again of God's faithfulness to open up doors of opportunity and provision each step of the way.

I am positive that Abraham's journey was no different than the faith journey you and I are challenged to take every day. God always instructs us in one way or another to, "Get out of your country, from your family and from your father's house, to a land that I will show you." He never gives us all of the details up front, but He expects us to take the first step before showing us how He will provide for all of life's "impossibilities."

I would encourage you today to be willing and obedient to the voice and leading of God. Dare to step out in faith in the direction God is calling you. He will never leave you stranded or without support, even if things look "impossible" to your rational mind. Instead, He will find ways and He will use people to Bless you and make you a blessing in the lives of those you meet along your way. God Is Good—All The Time!

Daily Declaration

I declare that I will continue to be sensitive to the voice and the leading of the Holy Spirit of God. I refuse to allow fear to keep me from entering into the purpose that God has planned for my life. I am a man/woman of faith, and faith always steps out into the unknown trusting God's Word and obeying His commands. Lord, I ask you to lead and to direct me in the paths of righteousness (See Psalm 5:8 and Psalm 23:3). Proverbs 3:5-6 instructs me to, "Trust in the LORD with all [of my] heart, and lean not on [my] own understanding; [6] In all [my] ways acknowledge Him [God], and He shall direct [my] paths." I trust in You Lord, and I place my life in Your care. Lead me Jesus and I will follow You. I pray all of this in Jesus' mighty name, Amen.

Day 10
Sacrificing Our Plans In Obedience To The Still Small Voice Of God

"¹¹ Then He said, "Go out, and stand on the mountain before the LORD." And behold, the LORD passed by, and a great and strong wind tore into the mountains and broke the rocks in pieces before the LORD, but the LORD was not in the wind; and after the wind an earthquake, but the LORD was not in the earthquake; ¹² and after the earthquake a fire, but the LORD was not in the fire; and after the fire a still small voice. ¹³ So it was, when Elijah heard it, that he wrapped his face in his mantle and went out and stood in the entrance of the cave…""

1 Kings 19:9-13 (NKJV)

How many times have you longed to hear God speak directly to you, just so that you knew that you were going in the right direction, making the right choices, and walking in line with His plans for your life? God is always speaking to us but we can miss what He is saying if we are not quiet and intent on hearing His still small voice through all of the worldly distractions.

In 1 Kings 19, Elijah has just defeated the prophets of Baal. Ahab the evil king gets word about what has happened and he tells his wife Jezebel, a false prophetess who has an axe to grind with the people of God. As a result, Jezebel vows to kill Elijah the following day.

Discouraged, Elijah leaves town fearing for his life. The next time we find him, he is sitting under a tree asking God to kill him. What has taken place in such a short period of time that would take Elijah from being extremely jubilant to utter despair? Elijah has just defeated 450 prophets of Baal and had them killed. God has made Elijah the victor over his adversaries and has in turn, reconciled the hearts of His people back to Himself—The True and Living God.

Doesn't it seem ironic that Elijah would become fearful of a threat made by a defeated queen? Isn't it unimaginable to think that after such a miraculous victory, Elijah would become discouraged, afraid, and ask God to kill him? We've got to remember however, that Satan always sneaks in, especially after our major victories, trying to convince us that what has just transpired was only a fluke. He wants us to believe that what we have just experienced was more the luck of the draw than it was a miracle of God. He will continually try to convince us that the next endeavor we embark upon won't turn out, won't end the same—that we've come to the end of our "luck." The important thing for us to remember is that we don't count on "luck" we count on God and His promises! But oftentimes after these kinds of victories, we are battle worn and have not yet refueled our faith in the Word, we begin to believe the lies of the enemy and doubt our ability in Christ Jesus.

As Elijah sits under the Juniper tree an angel appears to him and tells him to eat and drink food which he has miraculously provided for Elijah. The angel explains to him that God still has more work for him to complete. Elijah is told that He is to go to Mount Horeb (one of the mountain peaks of Mt. Sinai), the original place where God appeared to Moses as a burning bush and also the place where He gave him the Ten Commandments. Isn't it wonderful that when we are at our weakest, God always takes us back to the place in our lives where it all began? He takes us back to the place where we first encountered His power and His faithfulness, so that we can remember and continue to believe Him for our next victory.

The Bible tells us that when Elijah reaches Mt. Horeb, The Lord passes before him—probably the same way He passed before Moses when Moses asked to see God' glory (See Exodus 33:18). Then God speaks to Elijah in a still small voice and unveils the next part of His plan for Elijah.

When Patty and I left California to follow God's leading to go to Tulsa, our plan was to finish my degree at ORU and then move to Nashville, Tennessee. We made plans with family and friends detailing exactly how, when, and what we were planning to do. I told everyone that I would never move back to California. My plan was to visit our families once or twice each year, to get my beach fix during our visits, and to catch up with friends.

Even though I was born and raised in California, and even though California is a beautiful state with amazing weather year around, it has just never felt like home. Tennessee, Texas, and Oklahoma have always been my most favorite places to live and visit, even when I was just a kid. I just love the wide open spaces as opposed to the concrete jungle.

As I neared my graduation from Oral Robert's University, I sensed in my spirit a shift or a change. I wasn't sure exactly what it was, but I had always heard that if I wanted to hear God clearly, I needed to fast. I was desperate to make sure that we were making the right decision by moving to Tennessee, so I decided to start a fast and pray and ask if Nashville was still the plan that God had for us— or to determine if it had just been OUR PLAN?

Three days into the fast, I woke up at 1:22 am, went down stairs and began to pray. I had been waking up at that same time every morning yet I never set an alarm. Almost immediately, I began to hear in my spirit that we were to move back to California to plant a church in San Luis Obispo and another one in Monterey. As I already explained before, I didn't want to move back to California. Now what was I supposed to do? Obey God, or go my own way?

I remembered that Isaiah 1:19 says, "If you are willing and obedient, you shall eat the good of the land." I was neither willing, nor did I want to be obedient. In fact, I told God that morning that He was going to have to make it crystal clear that it was really Him speaking to me and not just anxiety about moving to Nashville, and starting all over again. I explained to Him that moving back to California didn't fit with my plans, that I had worked for years trying to leave California and only wanted to return for vacations. I was struggling with the idea of telling Patty what I thought God was speaking to my heart.

Two weeks later however, I came home from school to find Patty looking at homes on the internet in the San Luis Obispo area. I asked her if I had been talking in my sleep. Why was she looking at homes in California instead of in Nashville like we had originally planned? She explained that she felt like God was prompting her to get ready for a move to San Luis Obispo, and she couldn't shake that feeling.

I then explained to her what I believed God had said to me during my fast but told her that we still needed more confirmation before we set off back to California.

The next day I discovered that the pastor of the large television ministry I was working for was handing the church over to another minister. My position was no longer going to be needed, so I would need to find another job.

The following day, I received a call from Gary, a guy that I had previously worked with at the Medical/Pharmaceutical Company in California. I hadn't spoken with him in almost two years. When I answered the phone, he got right to his point, and asked if I would come back to work for them in California. He explained that he had three open territories and that I could choose which one I wanted. I thanked him but I wasn't interested. He urged me to at least hear him out and I agreed. He explained that the available territories included: San Luis Obispo, Monterey, and Fresno. To top it off, he would give me a large sign-on bonus and would pay all of our moving expenses back to California. He would also start me off at a higher base salary than the one I'd left. I knew this had to be a God thing but I still didn't want to go! I told him no thank you.

That night I couldn't sleep. I wrestled with the fact that beyond a shadow of a doubt this was God giving me the confirmations I had asked Him for. I finally blurted out, "Ok God, You win! I'll go back there if that's really where You want us to be."

The following morning I called Gary and signed all of the paperwork to begin my new job. What was I doing? I came to ORU for ministry not for a short-term escape from sales just to return again later. Was I missing God? Or was this all part of His plan? Though I had received the offer from Gary in January, my graduation wasn't until the end of April. I worked out the details with him to move back immediately after my graduation. The ball was rolling and leading us back to California, and the industry I had left when I decided to attend ORU. Yet my heart was still set on doing ministry, *NOT* on sales.

I arrived back in Fresno, Californian on May 2nd. Because it had been four months since I had accepted the job from Gary, He had decided that I would start out working the Fresno territory, and He would break me into the other areas at a later date. I immediately began experiencing great success within the first six months and converted about $5 Million in sales from my competitor. Patty and I soon began looking for homes to rent in the San Luis Obispo area which would allow us to keep our two medium sized dogs. I wasn't going to put down my dogs for any reason! That definitely wasn't part of God's plan!

Six months had passed and still no home in San Luis Obispo. I had applied for rental after rental but had no success in securing a home for our family. I had one agent agree to lease us a home but she called back the following day to explain that they had found another tenant without any pets and had decided to go with them instead! I was confused, frustrated, and felt trapped doing a job that I felt was a distraction from my calling in ministry.

One day as I was visiting my customers, I heard God speak to me again in that still small voice, telling me to turn off the sermon CD I was listening to and spend time with Him. I turned it off and felt as if God was instructing me to call Dr. Jerry Savelle's ministry. He said, "Get Brother Jerry to pray and agree with you according to Matthew 18:19-20 for a home in the San Luis Obispo area, and when you call him I want you to sow a $1000.00 financial seed into his ministry."

This wouldn't have sounded so strange except for the fact that I didn't know Dr. Savelle personally. Having worked in a large ministry in Oklahoma, I knew that Christians sometimes put preachers on pedestals and oftentimes act like groupies, trying to get as close as they can to them. I really didn't want to call his ministry and ask to speak to him—he didn't know me. Why would he take the time to speak to me? I also didn't want him, or any of his staff, to think that I was one of those weirdoes calling to bug a busy minister. After all, what was the chance that an evangelist with a global ministry would actually have the time to take my call? I knew that his schedule had him traveling all over the world approximately two-thirds of each month. But God interrupted my negative thinking and said, "Do you want YOUR breakthrough or not?!" I immediately answered back saying, "Yes, Sir I do! Please forgive me Lord."

I picked up my cell phone, called his ministry, explained that I was an ORU graduate hoping that would give me a little credibility, and that I was also one of his ministry partners—every little bit helped I guessed? I asked the receptionist if Brother Savelle ever took personal calls from his partners? I was transferred to his personal secretary who took my information and said that she would pass it along to him when he returned to the office. I thanked her and hung up the phone feeling extremely foolish.

I kept thinking to myself, *"Mike, that was the polite way of saying, 'Sorry, but Dr. Savelle doesn't take messages from fruit loop groupies.'"*

Three days later, on Saturday, March 17, 2006, my cell phone rang. I answered saying, "Hello, this is Mike." The voice on the other end of the phone said, "Hey Brother Mike, this is Jerry Savelle. I got a message that you called and I wanted to call you back and find out what you needed?"

I was stunned! Practically speechless! Dr. Savelle had been one of my long time heroes. I absolutely loved the way he preached faith and made the Bible come alive with his stories.

He explained to me that he was getting ready to fly out that afternoon for meetings in Australia, but he wanted to call me back first.

It may sound a little ridiculous, but even though I was now 36 years old my voice cracked like a teenaged boy going through puberty. Tears rolled down my face as I excitedly told him why I had called—maybe I was a weirdo groupie after all? We spoke for about twenty minutes. He prayed and agreed with me according to Matthew 18:19-20 for a home in SLO, and for the ministry we were about to launch. He ended our call by saying, "Well Brother Mike, I look forward to ministering with you one of these days in the near future."

I told him that God had instructed me to sow a financial seed into his ministry and asked if he wanted to take it by phone. He said, "No, I just wanted to call you back and pray with you. You can sow your donation online or mail it in, if you feel led by the Holy Spirit to do so."

"What a man of integrity!" I thought. He wasn't the least bit concerned with the offering, but was genuinely interested in speaking with me! I went online after hanging up the phone and sowed the seed.

I spent the next few weeks thanking God for His patience with me and for his amazing care in showing me that I really had heard His voice. I also repented for doubting Him! If I was honest, I had even been questioning and doubting whether I had really heard Him speak to me that first night back in Tulsa when He told me to move back to California.

Two days later however, there was no room for doubt. The prayer that I had prayed with Brother Savelle was answered. I received a call from the owner of a house I had found the same day that God told me to Call Jerry Savelle Ministries. I had filled out all of the paperwork and she called to notify us that the house was ours. We drove that day from Fresno to Morro Bay, finalized the deal, and scheduled movers for relocation to the San Luis Obispo area.

I learned a valuable lesson through that experience which has changed my life forever. I learned to be sensitive to God's leading and to never doubt my ability to hear His voice. Jesus said in John 10:27, "My sheep hear My voice, and I know them, and they follow Me." If we can hear His voice then that must mean that He is still speaking to us. The real question is, "Are we listening?"

I want you to know that as long as what we are hearing lines up with God's Word and can be established by two or three witnesses from Scripture, we can be confident that it is God speaking to us. I would encourage you to learn to sacrifice your own plans in order to experience God's best in your life. His plans are always better than our own because He knows the end from the beginning (See Isaiah 46:9-11), He has good plans to prosper us and to give us good success   (See Jeremiah 29:11) and He always has our best interests at heart   (See Jeremiah 31:3). Hallelujah! God is still speaking to His people today—Are you listening?

Daily Declaration

Heavenly Father, Today I am laying down all of my plans, all of my authority, and the entirety of my life at Your alter. I invite You to be my God and the Final Authority for my life. Father, speak to me and I will hear and obey Your voice. Jesus said that His sheep know His voice and that they follow Him (John 10:27). I am committed to my Lord Jesus and He is committed to me. Lord, I want to thank You for Your gentle and unending care for me. Thank You for loving me even when I fail to act as quickly as I should. Thank You for taking the time and for having the patience to walk me step-by-step through each and every process, and for confirming Your Word through the Bible, through people, and through direct encounters with You. Lord, I want to experience as much interaction with You as I am able to. I crave to hear You speak to me. I declare that I am sensitive to Your Spirit, to Your still small voice, and to Your presence. I will calm myself and learn to seek You each and every day. You are my life Jesus! Thank You for loving and speaking to me each day. I pray all of this in Jesus' name, Amen.

Day 11
On The Road Again: Destination Nashville

"^{23} And Jesus walked in the temple, in Solomon's porch. ^{24} Then the Jews surrounded Him and said to Him, "How long do You keep us in doubt? If You are the Christ, tell us plainly." ^{25} Jesus answered them, "I told you, and you do not believe. The works that I do in My Father's name, they bear witness of Me. ^{26} But you do not believe, because you are not of My sheep, as I said to you. ^{27} My sheep hear My voice, and I know them, and they follow Me."

John 10:23-27 (NKJV)

For the last two days we have been talking about hearing God's voice, trusting what you hear, and being obedient to follow His direction. Today I want to continue in that further. I know that some denominations teach that we cannot hear God's voice. They believe that those of us who talk about hearing God voice are egomaniacs that have made up those stories in order to deceive people into following us.

The good news for us is that I'm not the one who is telling you that we can hear the voice of God, but it was Jesus who said it in John 10:27, "My sheep hear My voice, and I know them, and they follow Me."

He also said that when His sheep hear His voice, they follow Him. It does **NOT** say that they follow His ministers. The last thing I want is for people to follow me. I am a man who makes mistakes but I always do my best to lead people to Jesus so they can follow Him.

We're in this together. If you are a born-again Believer, you have the ability to hear His voice and to follow Him. I can't live your life for you—only you can do that.

Still, if you want to hear God, you need to settle some things in your spirit for good. The first question you must ask yourself is, "Can I believe **ALL** of the Bible as God's Word and His will for my life?" If you answered yes to that question, then you'll never have to worry about debating over God's will for your life. It is settled once and for all by deciding that If God said it then that settles it! That is what it means to make God's Word the FINAL AUTHORITY for your life.

The second step is to make sure that you are not taking the Word out of context. The Bible tells us that our faith must be established by at least two or three witnesses from Scripture.

In 2 Corinthians 13:1 Paul warns hearers not to be deceived by others, and says, "This will be the third time I am coming to you. "By the mouth of two or three witnesses every word shall be established."

In Matthew 18:16 Jesus instructs us that when we confront a brother in sin, "That 'by the mouth of two or three witnesses every word may be established."

We learn from1 Timothy 5:18 "Do not receive an accusation against an elder except from two or three witnesses."

And Hebrews 10:28-29 tells us that when we refuse to accept Jesus as Lord of our lives, the judgment of eternal death comes upon us for rejecting those "witnesses," which are our PROOF of His Lordship according to the Bible. He goes on to say that because we have willfully rejected these Scriptural "witnesses" from the Bible, we have condemned ourselves. "[28] Anyone who has rejected Moses' law dies without mercy on the testimony of two or three witnesses. [29] Of how much worse punishment, do you suppose, will he be thought worthy who has trampled the Son of God underfoot, counted the blood of the covenant by which he was sanctified a common thing, and insulted the Spirit of grace?"

After moving to Morro Bay, California, we launched our church but California isn't part of the Bible-belt as you have probably already guessed. And after two and a half years of ministry I was still working bi-vocationally. I was spending about 60 hours each week working in my Medical/Pharmaceutical job which paid all of our bills, and about 20 to 30 hours per week doing ministry, promoting the church, leading Bible studies, and studying for my weekly sermon.

My heart was no different from any other pastor: I was determined to reach people and tell them what Jesus had made available to us through His death, burial, and resurrection, and to lead them to a personal relationship with Him.

Patty and I put over $150,000 of our own money into launching the church. Most of this money came from unexpected bonuses I received quite often for exceeding my sales goals, and from winning sales contests at work. We had many great people who were attending the church, many who are still close friends. In fact, I consider them more family than friends.

Many of the regulars gave selflessly to help support the vision that God had given to us and we learned together about God's faithfulness. I must admit I was pretty green when I first began preaching and these people were so gracious and generous to allow me to grow and even make some mistakes along the way.

I was so nervous during my very first sermon! I must have looked as pasty-white as a ghost. I was so scared that I would mess up that I was literally sick to my stomach. I thought that a good place to start teaching the people was to begin by preaching on the love of God.

As I walked up to the pulpit I saw that we had about 30 people in attendance. I started my message by telling a little joke, and then I became the joke—at least in my own mind. As I reached for my sermon notes, I knocked the music stand that I was using as a podium over twice within a five minute period. My notes went flying in different directions each time. I picked them up, tried to compose myself from embarrassment, and then proceeded to speed preach my message for what seemed like forever. I was certain that I had been talking for at least 45 minutes, but I was surprised that many of the people still looked at least half-engaged in what I was saying.

I ended my message, and invited everyone to stick around to get to know each other over refreshments. What I didn't know for a while was that my 45 minute sermon was really only about 5-7 minutes. I heard people whispering as they left saying things like, "Man that was the fastest church service I've ever been to!" I was sick to my stomach for the rest of the day, wondering if anyone would ever come back. I had lost my appetite and probably my congregation too Thankfully, many came back to give me another shot the following week, and thank God I was at least a little more calm preaching my message that time.

After four years of pastoring our church in San Luis Obispo, I woke up one morning and began praying and reading Bible. I had just returned from a church planter's conference out of state to help me learn new techniques to reach more people and to become more of a positive influence in our community. I felt in my spirit that we just weren't where I knew we were supposed to be. We had a number of regular attendees, but we had remained fairly steady in size for about a year or so. I knew that I needed help from "the experts." Unfortunately, seminary didn't teach us how to launch a successful ministry and keep it healthy and growing.

That morning as I was praying and asking God for His help and asking Him to Bless those who were already attending, and to bring the people who were supposed to be part of our church, I heard God say, "Now it is time to move to Nashville."

I was shocked; we hadn't finished what we had started in California. That had to be me! It must have been my frustrations, right? Why would God send us to Nashville, Tennessee now? It just didn't make sense!

I struggled with those thoughts for months all by myself. We had invested so much of our lives into these people and they had done the same with us. It didn't seem right to desert them when the going got a little tough or when I had become frustrated. Again, I didn't say anything to Patty because after all, we had only been back in   California for about five years. I decided to start another fast to make sure it was really God and not me. He spoke to me last time; He would speak to me this time too, if it was really Him. Wouldn't He?

My fast lasted almost three weeks. But all that I kept thinking about was, "I couldn't leave all of the people who'd spent the last four plus years believing with us to grow our ministry." But throughout those three weeks of fasting, I received Scripture after Scripture and confirmation after confirmation, that I was supposed to move my family to Tennessee to plant a church—even though it didn't make sense to my heart or my mind.

Five months passed as I wrestled with all of the guilt I was feeling. I was dreading the idea of telling our amazing members that we were leaving them and moving to Nashville. On top of that, how were we going to afford moving? Patty and I were putting every available dollar we had into keeping the church going and I had just emptied my savings account, buying more equipment and supplies. Now what?

I should have known that if God leads he also supplies the need. Once we took the first steps it all started falling into place, even though I was still struggling with my personal doubts.

It wasn't until, I went to a minister's conference in Fort Worth, Texas and heard the first speaker get up and begin preaching his sermon. A few minutes later he said something like, "There's someone in here that needs to hear the word Nashville. Then he went back to what he had been preaching beforehand. A good pastor friend of mine hit me in the arm and said, "There's more confirmation for you brother!" That was it! I couldn't deny God's leading any more. I went home to Morro Bay after that week-long minister's conference in Texas, knowing positively that we had to move to Nashville.

I broke the news to our congregation through tears and my own broken heart. Patty and I spent the next six months preparing for our move during which time God provided for us in many amazing ways. One of our closest friends and a member of our church blessed us with a large sum of money that she told me God had instructed her to give to us as a seed for our move to Nashville. She had just sold her home in Southern California, and the money was taken out of her profits from that sale. I still tear up thinking about how amazing God is and how awesome His people are.

On July 9th, 2010 I quit my job with the Medical/Pharmaceutical Company. People were telling me all over again that I was crazy to quit such a great job in a "down economy," but I knew that I had heard from God!

On July 10th I was a groomsman in my cousin's wedding. And on July 11th, 2010 Patty, our three kids, and I climbed into our car and pulling a trailer with our necessities, we began our three day drive to Nashville. We had no Idea where we were going to live, how we were going to eat and survive, or how quickly we would find jobs—but we were confident that God would provide.

We stayed with Patty's cousin for two days, and then with one of Patty's friends who had also just moved to Tennessee from Montana for a teaching job. Within a couple of weeks, we decided to move into an extended-stay hotel. Though it wasn't the most comfortable experience, cramming all five of us into a small one-room quarters, we knew that it was just a temporary thing.

Immediately, God began providing for us. I was asked by the hotel manager if I would be willing to work as night-time security four hours each night in exchange for a free room. I also began my doctoral program which had been launched by my spiritual mentor and spiritual father-in-the-faith, Kenneth Copeland. Within three months I got a job back in the Medical/Pharmaceutical industry. We soon moved out of the hotel and into an apartment just in time for our first Christmas in Tennessee. Since that time we have launched our ministry in Tennessee, and have moved into a new home that we were able to purchase. What an amazing journey it has been over the past few years.

Yes, there have been times of sacrifice but it has all been well worth it. We love Tennessee and our ministry is growing. We are looking to buy property in the near future to build a 6000 seat arena to minister to the community and to hold events that will be a Blessing to all of the people living here. The entire journey and all of the Blessings we have received are a testament to God's faithfulness to honor His Word. It has been an amazing experience to learn how to hear and to recognize God's voice. Though it has been difficult at times to walk by faith, learning to become willing to trust Him and to go in the direction He asks us to go, has been an amazing adventure. I can attest to the trustworthiness of 1 Thessalonians 5:24-25 which says, "[24] He who calls you is faithful, who also will do it. [25] Brethren, pray for us."

I want to thank you all for your prayers and for your continued faithful support of our ministry. The prayer of agreement mixed with faith always works!

Daily Declaration

Father, once again I thank you for speaking to me and for leading me in the direction that will be a Blessing for my life and for those around me. Lord, Your Word promises me, "When He, the Spirit of truth, has come, He will guide [me] into all truth; for He will not speak on His own authority, but whatever He hears He will speak; and He will tell you things to come." (John 16:13). You have also promised me that when You speak to me, I will have peace concerning the thing that You are telling me to do. 1 Corinthians 14:33 says, "For God is not the author of confusion but of peace..." Therefore, if I have an uneasy feeling in my spirit, if I am feeling any anxiety, fear, or confusion, and if I cannot find at least two or three witnesses from the Word of God that reinforce what I believe I am being directed to do, then I will wait until I have assurance that it is You and not the enemy trying to sabotage my life. At the same time, I understand that faith is spelled R-I-S-K, because faith always requires us to move out of our comfort zone and into uncharted territory. Faith stretches us and causes us to lean on You instead of our own abilities and knowledge. That being said, I understand that just because I may be experiencing a little timidity—if I can find Scriptures that illustrate that what I am being told to do has a Biblical foundation, I will move forward and   accomplish Your directives. 2 Timothy 1:7 says that You have not given me the spirit of fear, but of love, power, and a sound mind. I will not allow fear to keep me from doing anything You have called and equipped me to do. I can do **ALL** things in Christ who strengthens me (See Philippians 4:13). I am more than a conqueror in Jesus! (See Romans 8:37). And I am fully equipped to accomplish every task that You direct me to complete. (See 1 Corinthians 1:4-6, AMP). I thank You for Jesus and I pray all of this in His name, Amen.

Day 12
He's All Roar!

"⁶ Therefore humble yourselves under the mighty hand of God, that He may exalt you in due time, ⁷ casting all your care upon Him, for He cares for you. ⁸ Be sober, be vigilant; because your adversary the devil walks about like a roaring lion, seeking whom he may devour. ⁹ Resist him, steadfast in the faith, knowing that the same sufferings are experienced by your brotherhood in the world."

1 Peter 5:6-9 (NKJV)

When I think of a lion, I think of the most powerful, majestic, and the fiercest predator in the animal hierarchy. That is why the lion is known as the King of the jungle. He is at the top of the food chain and unafraid of anything. Jesus, our risen Lord and Savior, the Conquering King Of kings and Lord of lords is also known by another name, the Lion of the tribe of Judah. In Revelation 5:5 we read, "Do not weep. Behold, the Lion of the tribe of Judah, the Root of David, has prevailed to open the scroll and to loose its seven seals."

Have you ever noticed that whenever something is deemed valuable there are those who try to copy it? They are called counterfeiters or forgers. They try to mimic or pan themselves off as something they aren't. As a teen I occasionally would go to the L.A. Garment District. There we would find inexpensive deals on clothing and some of the latest fashions. As we would walk through the markets we would encounter people offering Rolex and other popular watches at ridiculously discounted prices. We could have bought ***what appeared to be the real deal*** for pennies on the dollar.

The problem was these items were knock-offs, fakes, and frauds that lacked the true quality, value, and character of the originals. Even though the outward appearance of these items was almost identical to that of the legitimate articles, something was missing in these counterfeits. A person who was familiar with the "real" could easily recognize the items being hocked here as fakes. Fakes don't just exist in the natural realm, but they also exist in the spiritual realm too!

In Isaiah 14:12-15 we learn that Lucifer, the devil, wanted to become god and to rule Heaven. The Bible tells us that he tried to exalt himself above God. "[12] How you are fallen from heaven, O Lucifer, son of the morning! How you are cut down to the ground, you who weakened the nations! [13] For you have said in your heart: 'I will ascend into heaven, I will exalt my throne above the stars of God; I will also sit on the mount of the congregation on the farthest sides of the north; [14] I will ascend above the heights of the clouds, I will be like the Most High.' [15] Yet you shall be brought down to Sheol, to the lowest depths of the Pit."

Satan tried to use the same tactics that God used when He created the world, to exalt himself above God, "[13] For you have said in your heart..."

Words are powerful, they have creative power within them, but the fake will never prevails over the REAL!

Satan has not stopped trying to attain a position above the ONE TRUE God. He is still trying to pawn himself off as something he is not. He is a counterfeit who continues to masquerade around and portray himself as being, "the king of the spiritual jungle." But for those of us who are familiar with, and have an intimate relationship with the True God of the universe, we can see right through his charade! We recognize that he is really lower than a dirt sucking worm!

1 Peter 5:8 warns, "[8] Be sober, be vigilant; because your adversary the devil walks about *like a roaring lion…*" If he is *like* a lion, then he's *not* a lion! He is only *impersonating* the Lion from the Tribe of Judah. Just like David who would have looked awkward if he had put on King Saul's armor to fight Goliath, Satan's appearance as a lion doesn't match his true identity—he doesn't have any authority except for the authority that we give him through our sin and unbelief!

In 1 Corinthians 11:14, we find Satan doing the same thing he is doing in 1 Peter 5:8. He is trying to convince us that he is more powerful that he really is and he is doing it through deception. He is trying to make us believe that he is an angel of light. But the truth is, he lost all of the light that was in him when he rebelled against God and was cast out of Heaven. There is no light in him, nothing righteous that would distinguish him as being filled with The Light—Jesus (See John 8:12, John 9:5, and 1 John 1:5).

The second thing we learn about the Devil from 1 Peter 5:8 is that he is, "seeking whom he *may* devour." If you are In Christ and abiding in the Secret Place of the Most High like Psalm 91 describes, then Satan may be seeking for you, but you are hidden, protected, and out of his reach. He will never be able to cause you any harm unless you get out from under that protection and open up a door to him through sin! In essence, when the enemy is prowling around like a lion searching for a way to "devour" you, God shuts his mouth like he did the lions in the pit Daniel was thrown into, and He says to him, "No, Satan, you *MAY NOT* touch my anointed!" (See Daniel 6:22). Hallelujah that is good news!

In 1 Peter 5:9, we are instructed to, "Resist him, steadfast in the faith, knowing…" The only way that we will be able to resist the Devil is by knowing what belongs to us IN CHRIST. By knowing what Jesus has made available to us through His death, burial, and resurrection. And by commanding the devil to flee when he has crossed the spiritual boundary line! Satan is tenacious and he doesn't give up easily. He does have authority, but only the authority that we allow him to have through our sin. When we stand in the righteousness we have in Jesus, covered by the blood, repentant of all sin, and hidden in the secret place, he can't harm us—he is powerless against us.

I encourage you today to recognize the fraud that Satan is. He is not all that he is portraying himself to be. The only real power he has is the power that we give to him. Draw near to God and His Word. Be quick to repent of any sin you may have committed. And resist every symptom, every negative attack, and every lie from the pit of Hell that he comes to you with, trying to convince you that he is the real deal.

Remember that under all of that veneer and shiny luster he's trying to convince you to buy into, he's only a worthless counterfeit—his lies won't last! If you're willing to believe and to stand on the truth of the Word of God—YOU can receive the VICTORY over every one of the enemy's lies. Satan's only a kitten pretending to be the king of the jungle! He's only an imposter trying to pawn himself off as the real thing. And in reality, he's ALL roar without any real power against you, unless you give it to him by sinning and not repenting of that sin. (See 1 John 1:9). When you blow it, be quick to repent. Humble yourself before the mighty hand of God, and then resist the Devil and he will flee from you—You've got God's Word on it!

Daily Declaration

Satan, I bind you in the name of Jesus! You are a liar! An imposter! And a worthless fraud! In fact the Bible says that you are a murderer, the Father of lies, and there is no truth in you. (See John 8:44). The Bible also tells me in Galatians 3:13-14 that I am redeemed from the curse through Jesus. I am not subject to any of the negative effects that sin would try to keep me in bondage to. In fact, Colossians 1:12-14 says that it is our Heavenly Father who has, "Enabled us to share in the inheritance that belongs to his people, who live in the light. [13] For he has rescued us from the kingdom of darkness and transferred us into the Kingdom of his dear Son [Jesus], [14] who purchased our freedom–and forgave our sins." I declare my freedom today in Jesus! I am no longer a prisoner to the lies of the enemy. I am no longer subject to the power of sin and the Curse. I am free to live fully, to enjoy my life, and to thrive in the Blessing of God, because I am IN CHRIST! Just like David declared in Psalm 13:6 (GWT) I can honestly declare, "I will sing to the LORD because he has been good to me." This is the day the Lord has made, I WILL REJOICE and be glad in it—in Jesus' mighty name, Amen.

Day 13
Multiplying Bacon

"^{41} And when He had taken the five loaves and the two fish, He looked up to heaven, blessed and broke the loaves, and gave them to His disciples to set before them; and the two fish He divided among them all. ^{42} So they all ate and were filled. ^{43} And they took up twelve baskets full of fragments and of the fish. ^{44} Now those who had eaten the loaves were about five thousand men."

Mark 6:41-44 (NKJV)

I believe in miracles! I believe that God is still performing miracles all around us as signs of His goodness and mercy in our lives. I believe that just as Jesus proclaimed there will be signs that follow our act of faith that will give witness to the fact that God has heard our prayers, has honored our faith, and is still at work setting the captives free. Jesus declared, "^{17} And these signs will follow those who believe: In My name they will cast out demons; they will speak with new tongues; ^{18} they will take up serpents; and if they drink anything deadly, it will by no means hurt them; they will lay hands on the sick, and they will recover." (Mark 16:17-18).

Let's turn our focus today to the first part of verse 17, where Jesus said, "And these signs will follow those who believe…" When we believe God, He expects us to receive a harvest on the things we have believed of Him. God created prayer between Him and man so that we would begin to see Him as our Source for all things, so that we would understand that it is His will to answer our prayers, and so we would interact with Him on a continual basis. Our job is to pray in faith believing that God has heard our prayer, and that He has answered our requests because of His great love for us.

1 John 5:14-15 promises, "[14] Now this is the confidence that we have in Him, that if we ask anything according to His will, He hears us. [15] And if we know that He hears us, whatever we ask, we know that we have the petitions that we have asked of Him."

When Jesus was ministering to a large crowd of people out in the wilderness, there was no place for them to go and get food to eat. Jesus had compassion for them and He told the disciples to bring what they had to Him so that they could be fed before being sent away. When the disciples surveyed the people, all that was found was two fish and five small loaves of bread.

For a group of 15,000 to 20,000 people (according to scholarly estimates which include women and children), it was only a drop in the bucket compared with the need they had to feed all of those who were present. In the disciple's eyes, two fish and five small barley loaves were worthless, but in Jesus eyes, that was more than enough! Those fish and loaves were a seed that He could work with. The small meal given by the young boy was a seed that Jesus could Bless, multiply, and use to feed everyone present, and still have more left over to give back to the boy who had given his seed as a love offering to God.

Jesus tells us that if we have faith the size of a mustard seed, we can do and receive more than we could ever imagine. The Message Bible uses a poppy seed as the example for this kind of faith, since most of us are more familiar with the size of a poppy seed than we are with the size of a mustard seed. Jesus said, "The simple truth is that if you had a mere kernel of faith, a poppy seed, say, you would tell this mountain, 'Move!' and it would move. There is nothing you wouldn't be able to tackle." (Matthew 17:20, MSG).

In other words, our faith in God's hands is limitless! There is absolutely nothing—and I mean NOTHING that is impossible when we dare to use our faith in combination with the promises of God. Do you believe that today?

Awhile back I stepped out in faith and left my career in the Medical/Pharmaceutical industry to follow my calling by going into full-time ministry. I believe that God was encouraging me to finally step out in faith and trust Him to meet all of my needs instead of trusting in my career or trusting in people. I had spent the past ten years working bi-vocationally, pastoring churches, doing some itinerant ministry and writing, while working simultaneously in the medical/pharmaceutical field.

In April 2013, God directed me to Matthew 10:7-10 and said to me, "I want you to trust me just like these men did when I told them to, "[7] ...Preach, saying, 'The kingdom of heaven is at hand.' [8] Heal the sick, cleanse the lepers, raise the dead, cast out demons. Freely you have received, freely give. [9] *Provide neither gold nor silver nor copper in your money belts, [10] nor bag for your journey, nor two tunics, nor sandals, nor staffs; for a worker is worthy of his food.*" (Emphasis Added).

It was those last two verses that God spoke to my heart. I believe that He was saying to me, "it's time that you quit resting in what you can do, what the company you have been working for can do, and begin resting in all that I have promised you that I would do for you as a covenant minister of My Word. I AM **YOUR** Source! Now do what I have called you to do, and I will do all that I have promised to do to meet all of your needs as one of My ministers."

His Words thrilled me yet at the same time I battled against the opportunity to fear. I have a home, automobiles, and bills like everyone else—and I needed to make sure that those bills were paid. How could I leave my career when in the natural, it "looked" as if we'd lose everything we owned and end up living on the streets?

God has truly Blessed us with some amazing and faithful partners who have given selflessly to this ministry, on a monthly basis. I also want you to know that God has been faithful to honor His Word to us. He is a Good God and everything He has promised us He has delivered! I truly believe that each of us needs to understand that when we step out into any faith endeavor, there will be times when God stretches us to believe Him for bigger things and will push us to accomplish greater feats by His grace.

For the past few months that is where I have been. It has been a good place to be and at the same time it has caused me to go deeper in His Word and into my prayer closet. I have had to stretch my faith muscles more than I ever could have imagined. In fact, there were times that my flesh felt like it couldn't possibly take any more stretching without the possibility of ripping completely apart. I have had to pray and praise my way through some things that didn't look like they would ever work out—but GOD IS FAITHFUL! I spent more nights than I care to admit, praying for BREAKTHROUGH just so we'd have gas to get back and forth and food on the table.

In fact, I was so determined to see God's promises come to pass in my life and ministry that I even embarked on a 40-day fast during the darkest days of that spiritual journey. I'm not saying this to discourage anyone, but to illustrate the fact that stepping out in faith is spiritual work that takes faith, determination, and an ALL-IN attitude that refuses to quit no matter the price or sacrifice!

Sometimes it can be work to rest in God when all Hell is breaking out all around you. It can be work to rest in His promises and allow Him to take the burden of all of your cares, and not go back to Him and try to take them back from Him. Many times we think we've cast our cares upon Him, only to find ourselves rushing back to try to help ourselves when it becomes uncomfortable. Sometimes the fear of failure grips us so hard that we want to scream, cry, and throw a fit, but we can't—we have to learn how to pray and praise our way through the storm—knowing that the "Son-shine" will dawn in the morning.

What I am going to say next may tweak your rational mind. It sure sent me reeling and questioning my sanity even though I believe in miracles as I stated in the beginning. But I believe that this true story will Bless you as much as it Blessed me?

One night during my 40 day fast, I had been up all night praying and praising God believing Him for my BREAKTHROUGH. I had been fighting fear over a financial attack I was under. Even though God had promised to meet all of my needs (See Philippians 4:19), I was overwhelmed by bills. My mortgage note was due and so were the bills for my Harley, and my wife's car. On top of that, many of my ministry partners had not yet sown their monthly donations like they had committed. It looked as if we might be late on all of our bills and possibly incur late fees too.

My wife got up at 4:30 a.m. to begin getting ready for her job. At 5 a.m. the kids woke up, took their showers, and began getting ready for school. I decided that I would make them breakfast, so I went to the fridge, grabbed some eggs, began peeling potatoes, and frying some bacon. As I was finishing up with the bacon I noticed that there was only one piece left in the package. Instead of putting it back in the refrigerator, I decided to cook it too. It was so thin you could practically see right through it. I used two thumbs to pull at the ends, making sure that it was only one piece and then put it in the pan to cook. When I grabbed the bacon with my tongs to flip it over and fry the other side, it suddenly turned into two pieces—what the heck just happened?

Immediately, inside of my spirit I heard God say to me, "That is what I am doing with everything you have been praying for. I'm multiplying your ministry, multiplying your opportunities, multiplying your finances, and multiplying your ministry reach! I AM Blessing everything that you are putting your hand to." (See Deuteronomy 12:7; Deuteronomy 15:10; and Deuteronomy 28:8, 12).

I instantly said out loud, "Lord, I receive it in Jesus' name!" My wife Patty, who was now doing her devotionals at the dining room table, asked me, "What are you talking about?" I explained to her what I had just seen and heard the Lord say to me, and she shouted, "I agree in the name of Jesus!"

Not ten seconds later, the enemy came to try to steal the Word which had been sown in my spirit by God Himself. Matthew 13:19 says, "When anyone hears the word of the kingdom, and does not understand it, then the wicked one comes and snatches away what was sown in his heart." Satan was trying to cause me to doubt that the bacon had just multiplied before my very eyes. He tried to intimidate me and make me feel foolish for thinking anything out of the ordinary had just occurred.

A voice in my head chuckled as it said, "That bacon didn't just multiply you moron!—It was just two pieces stuck together." Not two seconds later he came back with, "Jesus wouldn't multiply bacon—after all pigs are unclean animals—you idiot! Look how foolish you're being! To think that God would actually multiply bacon of all things—what a Bible scholar you are—Huh!"

Some of you may be thinking the same thing, but I know that I know, beyond a shadow-of-a-doubt, that God multiplied that bacon! I know God's voice and I know what I heard Him say to me. I also know how the enemy works to try to steal, to kill, and to destroy our faith in God's Word—our confidence in His reliability—and our perception about our identity IN CHRIST. You can laugh at me all you want, but honestly I don't care! I am free from the need or even the desire to try to prove myself or live up to what I believe people want me to be. My only concern is to please God, love my family and friends, and to be the best representation of Jesus that I can to everyone I meet.

I just hope that for those of you who still believe in miracles— that you can catch what Jesus said to me and begin to claim it for yourselves. God wants to Bless **Everything** that you put your hand to! There's no devil in Hell or in the earth that can stop us from living in Victory when God is on our side. Praise God!!!

We've also got to remember the vision that God gave to Peter in Acts 10:9-16 (NLT), "[9] The next day as Cornelius's messengers were nearing the town, Peter went up on the flat roof to pray. It was about noon, [10] and he was hungry. But while a meal was being prepared, he fell into a trance. [11] He saw the sky open, and something like a large sheet was let down by its four corners. [12] In the sheet were all sorts of animals, reptiles, and birds. [13] Then a voice said to him, "Get up, Peter; kill and eat them." [14] "No, Lord," Peter declared. "I have never eaten anything that our Jewish laws have declared impure and unclean." [15] But the voice spoke again: ***Do not call something unclean if God has made it clean.*** [16] The same vision was repeated three times. Then the sheet was suddenly pulled up to heaven."

Yes, I understand that this vision was referring to Peter's ministry to the Gentiles (the non-Jewish people), but the truth holds for bacon too. Although bacon is not something that we should eat every day especially if we want to remain healthy, the fact remains, if we bless our food before we eat it and ask God to keep us safe regardless of what we eat—He will do it.

In Acts 10:34 (KJV) Peter said, "Of a truth I perceive that God is no respecter of persons." The God's Word Translation says it this way, "Now I understand that God doesn't play favorites." In other words, if He is willing to Bless one person, He is willing to Bless any, and every other person who will believe His Word and trust Him to do what He has promised!

I believe that the bacon that multiplied in my frying pan, was a sign or a personal witness from God to me saying, "Mike, I AM still on My throne working on your behalf to complete the thing that I started in you." (See Philippians 1:6). He was saying to me, "Mike, I will not in any way fail you nor give you up nor leave you without support. [I will] not, [I will] not, [I will] not in any degree leave you helpless nor forsake nor let [you] down (relax My hold on you)! [Assuredly not!]'" (See Hebrews 13:6, AMP).

I believe God is using me today to remind you of this same truth! Your prayers have not gone unheard! They haven't been spoken in vain! Your praises are still ringing throughout all of Heaven, and God is sending His divine favor and His ministering spirits on assignment to bring you into your BREAKTHROUGH!

Keep hanging in there! Keep trusting God! Continue to persevere in your faith knowing that God is for you! Your answer is on its way to you right now! God never forgets His promises. He always follows through with the Word that He has spoken. Continue to fight the good fight of faith! The only reason it is a good fight—is because you have already been declared the VICTOR IN JESUS!

The battle never feels good to our flesh but when we win, it takes us to a whole new level of faith in Jesus. It makes the next battle we encounter a little easier knowing that if God brought us through the last one, He will certainly do the same thing with this one. Get your faith up and start believing for your breakthrough like never before. I don't know if it's the same where you are, but it's beginning to smell like a smokehouse where I'm living, because God is multiplying bacon!

Daily Declaration

Lord, I want to thank You for Your continued faithfulness in my life. I declare that my life is overflowing with Your goodness and I thank You that everything I put my hand to prospers! (See Deuteronomy 12:7; Deuteronomy 15:10; and Deuteronomy 28:8, 12). Like David said in Psalm 23:5-6, I can't help but to testify about Your divine favor at work in my life. "⁵ You prepare a table before me in the presence of my enemies; You anoint my head with oil; *my cup runs over. ⁶ Surely goodness and mercy shall follow me all the days of my life*; and I will dwell in the house of the LORD forever." (Emphasis Added). I love what David says about You Lord in Psalm 31:19-24 (GWT), and I echo his words testifying about You, "Your kindness is so great! You reserve it for those who fear [who worshipfully revere] You. Adam's descendants watch as You show it to those who take refuge in You. ²⁰ You hide them in the secret place of Your presence from those who scheme against them. You keep them in a shelter, safe from quarrelsome tongues. ²¹ Thank the LORD! He has shown me the miracle of His mercy in a city under attack. ²² When I was panic-stricken, I said, "I have been cut off from Your sight." But You heard my pleas for mercy when I cried out to You for help. ²³ Love the LORD, all you godly ones! The LORD protects faithful people, but He pays back in full those who act arrogantly. ²⁴ Be strong, all who wait with hope for the LORD, and let your heart be courageous." I pray all of this in Jesus' name, Amen.

Day 14
It's Raining Fish In Your Desert

"[16] And taking the five loaves and the two fish, He looked up to heaven and [praising God] gave thanks and asked Him to bless them [to their use]. Then He broke them and gave them to the disciples to place before the multitude. [17] And all the people ate and were satisfied. And they gathered up what remained over—twelve [small hand] baskets of broken pieces."

Luke 9:16-17 (AMP)

Most of us are familiar with the term, "It's raining cats and dogs," which simply means that the rain is really coming down. But you may be surprised to know that there are true stories which are verifiable by science, in which animals have reportedly fallen from the skies during heavy rains. This is not just an old wives' tale.

I recently heard a minister tell an odd story about an Australian village located approximately 500 miles inland from the coast. This little town is hundreds of miles from the nearest fresh water lake and situated in the middle of the outback (or desert region). The minister spoke about torrential showers which occurred in that area and of the hundreds of people who reported seeing fish raining down from the sky.

In amazement, I went to the internet to verify the story and found out that National Geographic and other reputable news sources had verified the veracity of the story. You can look it up for yourself at the following link: http://channel.nationalgeographic.com/wild/stranger-than-nature/videos/sky-fish/.

MICHAEL VIDAURRI, D. MIN.

You may be asking yourself, *"Why would you include such a peculiar story as the theme for a daily devotional?"* Well I'm glad you asked. Let me explain.

The Outback is a dry and typically waterless place. Though many people throughout the world live in desert areas, living conditions are harsh and food is often scarce—especially fish. In order for people to survive in such unforgiving environments they must take extreme precautions in order to insure that their environment doesn't end-up killing them.

The same is true for Believers. Once we have received Jesus as our Lord and Savior, He becomes our Source for everything. Acts 17:28 says about Him, "For in Him we live and move and have our being." Without His grace operating in our lives we couldn't even fill our lungs with oxygen to breathe. We could easily mimic the sentiment of the early reformer and martyr John Bradford who said, "But for the grace of God go I." In other words, if it wasn't for God's faithfulness and His grace none of us would have a chance at surviving in this life.

I have said all of this to make the point that even if you feel like your life resembles a desert, even if you are experiencing more month at the end of your money, and even if the news channels are predicting economic Armageddon—God is still our source! He is still our faithful God, Who has the ability to rain down exactly what we need, at exactly the right time, to get us through every storm that life can throw at us. Faith in Jesus and the promises He's made in the Bible is our lifeline—God is more than enough and His grace is sufficient. (See 2 Corinthians 12:9).

I can just see a couple of those villagers who experienced that crazy downpour of rain and fish talking to one another just prior to the storm saying, "Boy I'm getting tired of eating chicken, rabbit, and goat day in and day out. I wish we had some fresh fish to eat instead." The next thing you know, the two of them are praying in agreement according to Matthew 18:19-20, asking God for fresh fish, and voila! He begins raining fish down upon them, in answer to their prayers.

The scientists who studied this phenomenon believe that what happened was there was a waterspout (a tornado of sorts), which sucked up the fish from either the ocean or a lake 500 miles away, and then took them 60,000 to 70,000 feet into the atmosphere. They theorize that a strong gust of wind blew those fish inland to this remote village in the desert and rained them down in "the middle of nowhere." These scientists also theorize that most of the fish were still alive as they rained down to the ground, but some of them were slightly frozen. Talk about fresh seafood delivery! God is Good!

In the Bible fish always symbolize the Harvest. Jesus said to His disciples in Mark 1:17, "Follow Me, and I will make you become fishers of men." In the desert when He was ministering to the 5000 men and an estimated 15,000 women and children, He Blessed the two fish and the five loaves offered by the little boy and fed the entire multitude until they were satisfied. Then after everyone had finished eating the disciples collected twelve baskets full of leftovers (See Luke 9:16-17).

Do you remember the story when Jesus told Peter to go out fishing and said to him, "Cast in a hook, and take the fish that comes up first. And when you have opened its mouth, you will find a piece of money; take that and give it to them for [the Temple tax for] Me and you." (See Matthew 17:27).

God provided this same exact way for the Hebrews in the wilderness (which is another name for the desert). In Exodus 16:14 we read, "Then the LORD said to Moses, Behold, I will *rain* bread from heaven for you..." He rained down manna for them when they had nothing to eat.

Do you see that? He *rained* it down on them. God can and will use whatever method necessary to get you what you need—even if it means raining it down on you. Even if He has instructed another person to go to you and to give you the thing that you need and they aren't obeying what He's asked them to do. He still has a million and one methods to get you what you need. We've got to remember that

God is our Source—not people! But God will often use people to help meet our needs and then use us to help meet the needs of others. Praise God!

In Numbers 11:18-23 (NLT) we read the rest of the story about the Hebrews complaining to Moses for meat instead of Manna. If you remember God quickly became annoyed with their complaining and told Moses, "[18] Say to the people, 'Purify yourselves, for tomorrow you will have meat to eat. You were whining, and the LORD heard you when you cried, "Oh, for some meat! We were better off in Egypt!" Now the LORD will give you meat, and you will have to eat it. [19] And it won't be for just a day or two, or for five or ten or even twenty. [20] *You will eat it for a whole month until you gag and are sick of it*. For you have rejected the LORD, who is here among you, and *you have whined to him, saying, "Why did we ever leave Egypt?"' [21] But Moses responded to the LORD, "There are 600,000 foot soldiers here with me, and yet you say, 'I will give them meat for a whole month!' [22] Even if we butchered all our flocks and herds, would that satisfy them? Even if we caught all the fish in the sea, would that be enough*?" [23] Then the LORD said to Moses, "Has my arm lost its power? Now you will see whether or not my word comes true!" (Emphasis Added).

Did you notice how Moses responded to God's statement about giving everyone enough meat to eat over a 30 day period—so much meat in fact that they would gag on it and some would even die from gorging themselves?

To paraphrase Moses he said, "Even if we butchered all of our herds and even if you emptied the oceans of fresh fish, would it be enough to feed such a multitude of people?" The amazing thing is how God responded to Moses question. "*Is anything too difficult for God?*"

We've got to remember this when we are faced with our own crisis or "impossible" looking situations. Our bills, our need for healing, our need for whatever—is *NEVER* too difficult for the Creator of the Universe! He can and will provide whatever we need and desire, if we will just ask and believe Him for it in line with His Word.

Many Bible scholars believe that God brought the Hebrews quail every day, just like He rained down the fish in the Outback of Australia. They believe that He blew the quail in from the coastal areas where they lived, and rained them down upon the people, in order to fulfil His promise to them.

God is a Master at finding ways to fulfil His promises to His people. What promises are you believing Him for right now? Ask yourself the same question that God asked Moses "Is anything too difficult for God?" After answering that question for yourself, step out in faith, shut up with your complaining, and start believing Him for your answer. Then begin to look out and to look up—because it's about to start raining fish in your desert!

God can supply ALL of our needs in a million different ways! It doesn't matter where we live, it doesn't matter if He has to change government policies or Move Mountains to get us what He's promised us—He will do it!

The good news is that it only takes one of those million ways to get us everything we need, and to open up the door of His favor so that we can begin enjoying His more than enough Blessing in our lives. He can have someone Bless us with an unexpected gift. He can increase us through promotion on our jobs, or He can rain it down upon us simply because He loves us and has declared Himself as our covenant Source and supply for everything. Trust Him—believe BIG—and get ready for your supernatural harvest—I'm declaring to you right now that God is beginning to rain down fish in your desert today—In Jesus' Mighty Name! Amen!

Daily Declaration

I declare that the favor of God is raining down on me and all that concerns me in the name of Jesus! God You said in Malachi 3:10 (NIV) because I honor You with my tithe and offerings You will "Throw open the floodgates of heaven and pour out so much blessing that there will not be room enough to store it." Father I am a tither. I honor You in all that I have. And You are My covenant keeping God Who ALWAYS honors His Word. You know what my needs and desires are Lord, but I will list them before You now, knowing that You will intervene and rain them down on me because You Love me. Heavenly Father, in the name of Jesus I ask You for _____. Your Word says in Mark 11:24, "Therefore I say to you, whatever things you ask when you pray, believe that you receive them, and you will have them." And in 1 John 5:14-15 (AMP) You have promised saying, "[14] And this is the confidence (the assurance, the privilege of boldness) which we have in Him: [we are sure] that if we ask anything (make any request) according to His will (in agreement with His own plan), He listens to and hears us. [15] And if (since) we [positively] know that He listens to us in whatever we ask, we also know [with settled and absolute knowledge] that we have [granted us as our present possessions] the requests made of Him." I believe Your Word! I believe that You have heard and answered my prayers today. I receive everything that I have prayed for by faith. I thank You for Jesus! I thank You for making it clear to me, that it is Your will that I live a Blessed and Victorious life. I pray all of this in Jesus' name. Amen.

Day 15
Pay No Mind To The Wind

"[4] He who observes the wind [and waits for all conditions to be favorable] will not sow, and he who regards the clouds will not reap. [5] As you know not what is the way of the wind, or how the spirit comes to the bones in the womb of a pregnant woman, even so you know not the work of God, Who does all. [6] In the morning sow your seed, and in the evening withhold not your hands, for you know not which shall prosper, whether this or that, or whether both alike will be good."

Ecclesiastes 11:4-6 (AMP)

One of the questions we must ask ourselves consistently is: "Where is my focus leading me?" Did you know that we gravitate towards the things that we focus our attention on? When I was taking my motorcycle training courses so I could ride my Harley Davidson motorcycle safely, they continually warned us to keep our eyes focused in the direction that we wanted to travel. The instructors said, "You will gravitate in whichever direction your eyes are focused, even if the motorcycle is pointed straight in front of you. If you don't keep your eyes directed in the direction you want to travel—YOU WILL END-UP SOMEWHERE YOU DON'T WANT TO BE!

This statement is true for us spiritually as well! Distractions are all around and they continually try to take us off of our spiritual course. And when we pay too much attention to the wrong things, we often end up at the wrong destination.

The enemy knows that there is spiritual power that is released when we honor God with our tithes and offerings (our spiritual seed). Ecclesiastes 11:4-6 illustrates this point clearly. This Scripture tells us that no matter what happens in our lives, whether we have made it to our financial goals or not, there will always be some kind of "wind" that will be blowing, trying to convince us not to sow our seed. This is true even if we know and believe the promises of the Bible.

Examples of these types of winds include: talk of economic downturn, higher unemployment rates, or fears that there won't be enough for the things that we want and need. But just in case you've haven't noticed, the "winds" eventually die down and PEACE always returns.

2 Corinthians 5:7 (AMP) declares, "[7] For we walk by faith [we regulate our lives and conduct ourselves by our conviction or belief respecting man's relationship to God and divine things, with trust and holy fervor; thus we walk] not by sight or appearance."

As Believers we are not to be moved by our circumstances but we are to regulate our lives by the Word of God. I like the word regulate. It reminds me of a thermostat. When things get too hot, a thermostat kicks into action and goes to work cooling down the house to a comfortable temperature. When things get too cold, the thermostat kicks into gear and warms things up.

That is how our faith is designed to operate. We have been created to believe the things God has promised in His Word, regardless of how things "look." When we use our faith, based on the promises of the Bible, we can regulate or change our circumstances through believing, declaring, and standing on His Word. That's the point in which we become immoveable and untouchable by fear or any other "wind" that might be blowing our way.

Let me ask you another question. Do you know how God is going to answer every one of your requests? Of course not, but you believe that He will answer them, right? Well then, if you don't know how He's going to do it, then why would a little wind keep you from sowing your seed? Once your seed is in the ground the soil takes over and does exactly what it was designed to do. The only responsibilities left for us at that point, is to continue to water that seed and to pull all of the weeds that try to choke that seed and keep it from producing.

If that's the case (and it is), then how do we do this with the spiritual seeds we sow? We water and tend to those spiritual seeds with the Word of God.

Ephesians 5:26 describes a bride and groom's relationship similar to the relationship between Jesus and the church. This passage talks about the wife submitting to the husband as the head of the family just as the Church submits to Jesus as the Head of the Church. When this kind of submission takes place in the spirit of love, the Bible says that Jesus is able to sanctify (set apart), cleanse, and wash us, "with the washing of water by the word." (Ephesians 5:26, KJV). When we learn to put the Word of God above everything else, it protects and provides for all of our needs. The Word nourishes and quenches all of our spiritual hunger. The Bible is real SPIRIT and SOUL FOOD! Amen!

Proverbs 3:1-10 says, "[1]My son, do not forget my law, but let your heart keep my commands; [2] for length of days and long life and peace they will add to you. [3] Let not mercy and truth forsake you; bind them around your neck, write them on the tablet of your heart, [4] and so find favor and high esteem in the sight of God and man. [5] Trust in the LORD with all your heart, and lean not on your own understanding; [6] in all your ways acknowledge Him, and He shall direct your paths. [7] Do not be wise in your own eyes; fear [worshipfully respect] the LORD and depart from evil. [8] It will be health to your flesh, and strength to your bones. [9] Honor the LORD with your possessions, and with the first-fruits of all your increase; [10]

so your barns will be filled with plenty and your vats will overflow with new wine.

Proverbs 4:20-22 declares, "[20] My son, give attention to my words; incline your ear to my sayings. [21] Do not let them depart from your eyes; keep them in the midst of your heart; [22] *For they are life to those who find them, and health to all their flesh.*" (Emphasis Added).

Now look at what Matthew 14:22-32 tells us, "[22] Immediately Jesus made His disciples get into the boat and go before Him to the other side, while He sent the multitudes away. [23] And when He had sent the multitudes away, He went up on the mountain by Himself to pray. Now when evening came, He was alone there. [24] But the boat was now in the middle of the sea, tossed by the waves, for the wind was contrary. [25] Now in the fourth watch of the night Jesus went to them, walking on the sea. [26] And when the disciples saw Him walking on the sea, they were troubled, saying, "It is a ghost!" And they cried out for fear. [27] But immediately Jesus spoke to them, saying, "Be of good cheer! It is I; do not be afraid." [28] And Peter answered Him and said, "Lord, if it is You, command me to come to You on the water." [29] So He said, "Come." And when Peter had come down out of the boat, he walked on the water to go to Jesus. [30] But when he saw that the wind was boisterous, he was afraid; and beginning to sink he cried out, saying, "Lord, save me!" [31] And immediately Jesus stretched out His hand and caught him, and said to him, "O you of little faith, why did you doubt?" [32] And when they got into the boat, the wind ceased."

What would have happened if Peter never stepped out of the boat and used his faith to walk out to Jesus? He never would have walked on the water! He would have allowed the "wind" and his circumstances to control his destiny. What happened immediately after Peter and Jesus got back into the boat? The "WIND" ceased!

The "wind" is always there to discourage us and to deter us from stepping out of our spiritual boats and reaching our full-potential IN CHRIST JESUS. Some people call the wind—The Fear of the   Unknown. No matter what we call it—IT'S FEAR—And God didn't give us the SPIRIT OF FEAR! No! God gave us the Spirit of POWER, the Spirit of LOVE, and the Spirit of a SOUND and FAITH-FILLED MIND! (See 2 Timothy 1:7). The advantage that Believers have over the World is that with God, we always know the outcome—and it's ALWAYS THE BLESSING!

Don't allow the "wind" to keep you in your spiritual boat. Don't allow the wind to keep you from sowing your seed and reaching your destination. And don't allow the "wind" to keep you from prospering in THE BLESSING of God! We may not know exactly how God is going to accomplish the things He has promised, but we have His covenant promises that He will do it! Remember, no matter how hard the "wind" is blowing, if you are obedient to obey Him and step out of your boat and onto His promises, the wind will eventually die down and you'll experience greater things than you could have ever imagined. Obey God, trust in His promises, and sow your seed!

Daily Declaration

I declare that no "wind," no devilish plot, and no fear will keep me from obeying God. I am a doer of the Word of God and I sow my seeds in faith knowing that God will pour out His Blessing upon me in abundance. Lord, You told me in 2 Corinthians 9:6-9 (AMP), "[6] [Remember] this: he who sows sparingly and grudgingly will also reap sparingly and grudgingly, and he who sows generously [that blessings may come to someone] will also reap generously and with blessings. [7] Let each one [give] as he has made up his own mind and purposed in his heart, not reluctantly or sorrowfully or under compulsion, for God loves (He takes pleasure in, prizes above other things, and is unwilling to abandon or to do without) a cheerful (joyous, "prompt to do it") giver [whose heart is in his giving]. [8] And God is able to make all grace (every favor and earthly blessing) come to you in abundance, so that you may always and under all circumstances and whatever the need be self-sufficient [possessing enough to require no aid or support and furnished in abundance for every good work and charitable donation]." Hallelujah! I believe it, I receive it by faith, and I sow my seed to You and towards the work of Your Kingdom in Jesus' name, Amen.

Day 16
Rest Is An Attitude Of Faith

"[9] There remains therefore a rest for the people of God. [10] For he who has entered His rest has himself also ceased from his works as God did from His. [11] Let us therefore be diligent to enter that rest, lest anyone fall according to the same example of disobedience. [12] For the word of God *is* living and powerful, and sharper than any two-edged sword, piercing even to the division of soul and spirit, and of joints and marrow, and is a discerner of the thoughts and intents of the heart."

Hebrews 4:9-12 (NKJV)

What is rest? Is it taking a vacation and lounging around in a hammock and reading a good book? Is it taking a nice nap during the afternoon because you don't have any pressing business to complete? Or is rest an attitude of faith, knowing that once you have cast all your cares onto God, He is faithful to carry you through all of life's storms unscathed?

You see, it is often our intention to hand the weight of our circumstances over to God after we have prayed and asked Him to help us. But because of unbelief and fears that He hasn't heard us, or that he might not answer us, we usually tend to take the weight of our burdens back from Him, and try to handle them ourselves. The root cause of this behavior is our lack of confidence and understanding of His willingness to help us. It all stems from fear and unbelief.

We're not the only ones who have struggled with this type of unbelief. In fact, 1 Corinthians 10:1-13 (NLT) explains that all humanity struggles with unbelief because of the sin that has been passed down from our spiritual parents, Adam and Eve. "[1]I don't want you to forget, dear brothers and sisters, about our ancestors in the wilderness long ago. All of them were guided by a cloud that moved ahead of them, and all of them walked through the sea on dry ground. [2] In the cloud and in the sea, all of them were baptized as followers of Moses. [3] All of them ate the same spiritual food [manna], [4] and all of them drank the same spiritual water [from the rock Moses struck in the desert]. For they drank from the spiritual rock that traveled with them, and that rock was Christ. [5] Yet God was not pleased with most of them, and their bodies were scattered in the wilderness [6] These things happened as a warning to us, so that we would not crave evil things as they did, [7] or worship idols as some of them did. As the Scriptures say, "The people celebrated with feasting and drinking, and they indulged in pagan revelry." [8] And we must not engage in sexual immorality as some of them did, causing 23,000 of them to die in one day. [9] Nor should we put Christ to the test, as some of them did and then died from snakebites. [10] And don't grumble as some of them did, and then were destroyed by the angel of death. [11] These things happened to them as examples for us. They were written down to warn us who live at the end of the age. [12] If you think you are standing strong, be careful not to fall. [13] The temptations in your life are no different from what others experience. And God is faithful."

There are two crucial points to these verses—each of these examples are about people who have blown it and paid a price for their sin. These stories are EXAMPLES that God has given to help keep us from making the same mistakes. They are a witness that sin always demands a price and whether you know it or not, unbelief is a sin! Romans 14:23 tells us, "For whatever is not from faith is sin." The most important point that we can take from this passage is that, we have no reason to fear anything because GOD IS FAITHFUL to do all He has promised! God is faithful to take care of all our needs and desires when we cast our cares onto Him—we can count on it!

In Psalm 62:1-2 (NCV) we read, "I find rest in God; only he can save me. [2] He is my rock and my salvation. He is my defender; I will not be defeated." This is the true posture of resting in faith. Faith knows that no one has your best interest at heart more than God! Faith trusts and rests in God's promises knowing that it will all work out in your favor—because God has promised to care for all of your needs and desires! He is your covenant partner and your God.

You may be facing the most difficult days of your entire life right now. Your circumstances may look "impossible" to solve, BUT GOD IS FAITHFUL! It may look like you'll never find another job, and like the bills will never stop piling up, BUT GOD IS FAITHFUL! Your kids may be acting like fools, BUT GOD IS FAITHFUL! There may be too much week at the end of your money, BUT GOD IS FAITHFUL!

No matter what you are facing, your problem is never too BIG for God! If you can find the faith to cast your cares over on Him and allow Him to deal with them from this moment forward—God will make a way and get you to the other side of your mountain! He really does care for YOU. He loves us more than we could ever imagine. And He is willing to take over the responsibility of making things right in our lives. He will make them better than they have ever been. Trust Him—Lean on Him and His strength as Almighty God—and **REST** by taking comfort in His ability as your Source and Supply for ALL of your cares and concerns today.

Proverbs 3:5-8 (ERV) says, "[5] Trust the LORD completely, and don't depend on your own knowledge. [6] With every step you take, think about what he wants, and he will help you go the right way. [7] Don't trust in your own wisdom, but fear and respect the LORD and stay away from evil. [8] If you do this, it will be like a refreshing drink and medicine for your body."

Resting in God doesn't mean that we become flaky and throw all reason out of the window. No, we have the responsibility to cast our care onto Him and then rest in our faith by building ourselves up on the Bible promises concerning our requests.

If we need healing in our body then we rest by speaking healing Scriptures over ourselves. If we are believing for a financial miracle, then we meditate on the Scriptures which promise us that He will provide for our needs. We still have work to do when we cast our care onto God, but that work consists of keeping our eyes on Him and encouraging ourselves in His Precious Promises. Otherwise we will quickly fall back into unbelief even if we have experienced His faithfulness before.

We've got to remember that God's Word is not just an old book that we read to comfort ourselves—THE WORD is ALIVE! In fact, Hebrews 4:12 (AMP) says, "For the Word that God speaks is alive and full of power [making it active, operative, energizing, and effective]; it is sharper than any two-edged sword, penetrating to the dividing line of the breath of life (soul) and [the immortal] spirit, and of joints and marrow [of the deepest parts of our nature], exposing and sifting and analyzing and judging the very thoughts and purposes of the heart." In other words, we aren't recklessly placing our faith in a dead God, but we are resting in the fact that He is a LIVING, POWERFUL, FAITHFUL, and LOVING God, who is working out everything we need Him to, because He cares for us!

Hebrews 3:8-14, 17-19 tells us, "[8] Do not harden your hearts as in the rebellion, in the day of trial in the wilderness, [9] Where your fathers tested Me, tried Me, and saw My works forty years. [10] Therefore I was angry with that generation, and said, 'They always go astray in their heart, and they have not known My ways.' [11] So I swore in My wrath, 'They shall not enter My rest.'" [12] Beware, brethren, lest there be in any of you an evil heart of unbelief in departing from the living God; [13] but exhort one another daily, while it is called "Today," lest any of you be hardened through the deceitfulness of sin. [14] For we have become partakers of Christ if we hold the beginning of our confidence steadfast to the end...[17] Now with whom was He angry forty years? Was it not with those who sinned, whose corpses fell in the wilderness? [18] And to whom did He swear that they would not enter His rest, but to those who did not obey [believe and act on His promises]? [19] So we see that they could not enter in because of unbelief."

These people witnessed God do the impossible in their lives. They saw Him open up the Red Sea and create a safe passage of escape from the Egyptians who were trying to recapture and kill them. But God was faithful to His promise to deliver them from their enemies. The Egyptians chased the Hebrews into the sea and followed after them on the dry ground that God had provided for them to escape. As the last Israelite reached the other side of the sea, the Egyptians were swallowed up by the sea and drowned.

These same people witnessed the glory of God as He brought forth water from a rock in the middle of the desert. They witnessed God's supernatural cloud by day which protected them from the excruciating heat by day and His pillar of fire by night which provided light so that they could see their way. God was their All-in-All for forty years as they wandered through the desert, yet they continued to doubt and complain against Him—forgetting to thank Him for all that He'd done to Bless and care for ALL of their needs.

What has God done for you? Can you remember anything that He's done for you recently? Or are you taking Him and His unmerited favor in your life for granted?

Take a moment now to thank Him for all He has done for you this week. He's given you breath in your lungs. He's provided food for your nourishment. He's kept you strong and healthy. He has protected your family and your home. He has done amazing things for you already. Isn't it time to give Him praise for all those things he's provided and to say, "Lord, since you have proven yourself faithful in all these things, I will rest confidently in You, knowing that everything I have handed over to You, You will do for me because You love me. Thank You for taking care of me and for loving me beyond all that I deserve! I love You Father, You are My Amazing God!

Daily Declaration

Father, I am thankful that I have found my rest in You. I echo the words of David from Psalm 62:5-12 (ERV) by saying to You today, "I must calm down and turn to God; He is my only hope. [6] He is my Rock, the only one who can save me. He is my high place of safety, where no army can defeat me. [7] My victory and honor come from God. He is the mighty Rock, where I am safe. [8] People, always put your trust in God! Tell him all your problems. God is our place of safety. Selah [9] People cannot really help. You cannot depend on them. Compared to God, they are nothing—no more than a gentle puff of air! [10] Don't trust in your power to take things by force. Don't think you will gain anything by stealing. And if you become wealthy, don't put your trust in riches. [11] God says there is one thing you can really depend on, and I believe it: "Strength comes from God!" [12] My Lord, your love is real. You reward all people for what they do [You reward people for placing their trust and their hope in You]."

Lord, I cast all of my cares over to You and refuse to take them back from out of Your caring arms. I recognize and receive all of the Love that You have for me. You don't just have love for me—You ARE the purest form of LOVE—You are *El Shaddai*—My God Who is More Than Enough! Thank You Father! I pray all of this in the mighty name of Jesus. The name above every name and circumstance I could ever face. I love You Lord, Amen.

Day 17
What Are You Thinking?

"⁸ Finally, brethren, whatever things are true, whatever things
are noble, whatever things are just, whatever things are pure,
whatever things are lovely, whatever things are of good
report, if there is any virtue and if there is anything
praiseworthy—meditate on these things."

Philippians 4:8 (NKJV)

Your thoughts are the blueprint or the building blocks for
your life. Everything in life originated with a thought.
Before God created anything, He first had an idea, and He
gave life to that idea through His spoken Word.

Hebrews 11:3 declares, "By faith we understand that the worlds
were framed by the word of God, so that the things which are seen
were not made of things which are visible."

Psalm 33:6 states, "By the word of the LORD the heavens were
made, and all the host of them by the breath of His mouth." But our
God is not a God of chaos, He is a God of order and therefore, He
knew what He wanted to create before He ever started.

We learn a wonderful Biblical truth from Proverbs 23:7 which
explains, "For as he thinks in his heart, so is he." This is great for the
Believer and non-believer alike, because it leaves the outcome
completely up to us. We can decide how we want to live and then set
our course based on our decisions. This is an example of the free-
will that God has given to humanity. In essence, He is saying, "I am
giving you the opportunity to create your own life just as I created
the world and everything in it—through your purposeful decision to
become or to reject all that you desire—You Choose!

I love Dr. Creflo Dollar's explanation of the progression from our thoughts to living out those realities. He says that everything begins with one's thoughts, which lead to words, which create emotions, which lead to decisions, which produce actions, which create habits, which form one's character, and ultimately leads to one's destiny.

In his book *8 Steps to Create the Life You Want: The Anatomy of a Successful Life*, Dollar writes, "Part of the process of reaching your destination and being successful is recognizing that you have a part to play. So many people 'wait on God' to take them to their place of fulfillment in life, and then blame Him when they fail. Others consider the Bible to be some sort of magic book of promises. They want only to name it and claim it, believe it and receive it, then go, 'Poof...there it is!' But there's so much more! People who think this way somehow convince themselves that God will magically fix their situation. Here's a news flash: God isn't into magic tricks! He has a master plan and your job is to operate within that plan. There are also people on the opposite extreme. They don't see the need to get God involved in their decisions at all. Rather than seeking Him for guidance, they rely on their experience, education, and networking skills to lead them to the path of success. I often hear people say, 'What's meant to be will be,' but that just doesn't line up with Scripture. Your decisions are what create your reality; nothing just happens. The truth is, until you identify God's plan for your life and understand the process that leads to your destination, you will either delay or forfeit the good life He has planned for you."

It's these reasons that we carefully guard our thoughts and ultimately our spirit by choosing what we want in life and refusing to settle for anything less than God's best. Our Heavenly Father has given us the prescription to creating a life beyond measure through obeying His Word. Philippians 4:8 instructs us saying, "Finally, brethren, whatever things are true, whatever things are noble, whatever things are just, whatever things are pure, whatever things are lovely, whatever things are of good report, if there is any virtue and if there is anything praiseworthy—meditate on these things."

Did you notice that everything in that list is the opposite of what the devil continually tries to convince us to believe and receive as the truth for our lives? Each and every one of those things that Paul listed in Philippians 4:8 are things that connect us to God's goodness and His BLESSING! God wants us to LIVE IN HIS BLESSING and to EXPERIENCE HIS ABUNDANT LIFE!

I encourage you to follow the advice of Philippians 4:8 and to guard your thoughts from the lies of the enemy. You have the final say in YOUR life regarding how you will live, what you will receive, and what you will reject in this earth. Matthew 18:18-19 (AMP) promises us, "[18] Truly I tell you, *whatever you forbid and declare to be improper and unlawful* on earth must be what is already forbidden in heaven, *and whatever you permit and declare proper and lawful* on earth must be what is already permitted in heaven. [19] *Again I tell you, if two of you on earth agree (harmonize together, make a symphony together) about whatever [anything and everything] they may ask, it will come to pass and be done for them by My Father in heaven*." (Emphasis Added).

When the enemy comes at you with thoughts of doubt, defeat, fear, or sickness, tell him that those aren't your thoughts! Rebuke him in the name of Jesus! Then command him to flee from you according to James 4:7. Then begin to meditate on the promises from God's Word, which are true, noble, just, pure, lovely, good, virtuous, and praiseworthy, and begin creating all of the great things God has for you and your family TODAY!

Daily Declaration

I declare that I will only think on things which are true, noble, just, pure, lovely and of a good report—I will meditate only on things that are praiseworthy. I declare that I have a sound mind, a healthy body, and a prosperous and BLESSED life! I have been redeemed from the Curse through Jesus. I am fully   persuaded that My Heavenly Father loves me and will take care of all my needs because I have committed my life to Him! Jesus, I invite You to lead, direct, and guide me through this life. Your plan for me is better than any plan I could ever create on my own. Holy Spirit, speak to me, and show me Your will for my life. I will correct anything that You instruct me to correct and I will obey Your Words immediately. I choose to be clay in Your hands, for you are the Master Potter. Isaiah 64:8 says, "Yet, O Lord, You are our Father; we are the clay, and You our Potter, and we all are the work of Your hand." I declare that my mind is alert and my heart is receptive to Your Holy Word. Speak Lord, and I will do as You request. Father, I commit to do all that You directed Joshua to do in Joshua 1:8 (AMP), so that I can guard my thoughts, guard my spirit, and have good success. "This Book of the Law shall not depart out of your mouth, but you shall meditate on it day and night, that you may observe and do according to all that is written in it. For then you shall make your way prosperous, and then you shall deal wisely and have good success." I pray all of this in Jesus' name, Amen.

Day 18
Your Success Is Determined By YOU!

"⁸ This Book of the Law shall not depart from your mouth, but you shall meditate in it day and night, that you may observe to do according to all that is written in it. For then you will make your way prosperous, and then you will have good success. ⁹ Have I not commanded you? Be strong and of good courage; do not be afraid, nor be dismayed, for the LORD your God *is* with you wherever you go."

Joshua 1:8-9 (NKJV)

The Bible is FAITH FOOD! It is fortified with EVERY spiritual nutrient available. Look at what this passage is saying. We are to have the Word in our mouths continually. We need to be speaking it, meditating on it, [chewing on it, getting out every bit of valuable nutrient that is within], and living it out.

The Book of James says it this way in James 1:21-22, "²¹ Therefore lay aside all filthiness and overflow of wickedness, and receive with meekness the implanted word, which is able to save your souls. ²² But be doers of the word, and not hearers only, deceiving yourselves." Hearing is not enough! Faith comes by hearing (Romans 10:17), but we need to do more with the Word than just hear it. We need to apply what we're hearing, and then put God's principles to work in our lives!

When we speak the Word, meditate on the Word, and become living epistles displaying God's Word in action—prosperity and success are the natural by-product. They come automatically.

Why? Because the Word is connected to the BLESSING! The Word of God is the creative force through which everything in this universe was made (Hebrews 11:3).

Jesus is the Word incarnate. Jesus is the Word who became flesh (John 1:1-5). And Jesus never minced His words. He said exactly what He heard The Father say (See John 5:19, 30; John 7:18; John 12:49-50). He said what He wanted, and He received what He said.

If you want prosperity in every area of your life, if you want success, follow Jesus' pattern. Become a man or woman of the Word! By doing so, YOU make your way prosperous and then YOU will have good success. (See Joshua 1:8).

There will be times when things don't look like they are working, but stick with the Word. This is the time when you need to become steadfast [planted in your faith], trusting God to do what He's promised He'd do. It takes courage and focus to live by faith! Especially when you're facing surmounting obstacles and pressure, it's easy to give up and quit. But VICTORIOUS Believers don't give up when things get tough—they continue to fight the good fight of faith until they can show the world that they are More Than Conquerors IN CHRIST!

Paul said it this way in Hebrews 10:38-39 (AMP), "[38]But the just shall live by faith [My righteous servant shall live by his conviction respecting man's relationship to God and divine things, and holy fervor born of faith and conjoined with it]; and if he draws back and shrinks in fear, My soul has no delight or pleasure in him. [39]But our way is not that of those who draw back to eternal misery (perdition) and are utterly destroyed, but we are of those who believe [who cleave to and trust in and rely on God through Jesus Christ, the Messiah] and by faith preserve the soul." So don't draw back, cave in, and quit. Work the Word and the Word will work for you!

You Are The Determining Factor In YOUR Faith Journey. Will YOU give up and quit, or will YOU stick it out with God, Declare the Word in faith, and Reach YOUR Divine Destination? YOUR SUCCESS IS DETERMINED BY YOU! Jesus Is Lord!

Daily Declaration

I declare that I have victory over sin, sickness, and every effect of the Curse—In Jesus Mighty Name! I am More Than A Conqueror In Christ! I am the head and not the tail (See Deuteronomy 28). I am above and not beneath. My God has BLESSED me with every spiritual BLESSING IN CHRIST (See Ephesians 1:3). Job 22:28 (AMP) promises, "You shall also decide and decree a thing, and it shall be established for you; and the light [of God's favor] shall shine upon your ways." I am determined to speak ONLY what the Father has spoken to me in His Word. I CHOOSE LIFE because I CHOOSE JESUS and His plan for me. Heavenly Father You have set death and life before me, Blessing and Cursing, and I consciously Choose Life (See Deuteronomy 30:19). I receive Your divine favor and the light of Your Goodness. Thank You for loving me and for giving me the opportunity to live the Abundant Life in Jesus! Jesus came for one purpose—to free me and the rest of humanity from the bondage of sin. He came to restore my relationship with You Father. I am grateful for Jesus! I receive by faith the life He came to provide for me: a life that I can enjoy, and a life that is abounding and overflowing with Your love and immeasurable BLESSING (See John 10:10, AMP). I pray all of this in Jesus' name, Amen.

Day 19
Live BLESSED!

"Blessed be the God and Father of our Lord Jesus Christ, who has blessed us with every spiritual blessing in the heavenly places in Christ"

Ephesians 1:3 (NKJV)

How does it feel to know that you have all that you could ever possibly want or desire at your disposal because of who you are connected to? That is right! Your relationship with Jesus, has given you access to every benefit and Blessing that He took back for us on the cross. In other words, you have been redeemed from the curse of sin, the curse of sickness, poverty, lack, and eternal separation from God.

Galatians 3:13-14, 29 say it this way, "[13] Christ has redeemed us from the curse of the law, having become a curse for us (for it is written, "Cursed is everyone who hangs on a tree"), [14] that the blessing of Abraham might come upon the Gentiles in Christ Jesus, that we might receive the promise of the Spirit through faith…[29] And if you are Christ's, then you are Abraham's seed, and heirs according to the promise." Amen! You have an inheritance!

Does this mean that God is your personal genie in a bottle? Does it mean you and I can order God around like we do our children, expecting Him to answer our every command? Of course not! However, it does mean that if you can find a promise in the Scripture; then it is yours! The only requirements are that you believe and act on what He has told YOU to do. Receiving answers to prayer requires faith and obedience of faith and obedience. I'm not talking about a works based religion. I'm talking about an understanding of what belongs to us as heirs to God's promises in the Bible through Christ—our High Priest and Mediator.

Jesus promised in John 14:14-15, "[14] If you ask anything in My name, I will do it. [15] "If you love Me, keep My commandments." Blessing comes to us as a result of walking in love, operating by faith, and living in obedience to God's Word.

Isaiah 1:19 tells us, "If you are willing and obedient, you shall eat the good of the land." Willing to do what? Willing to do what is required by God in order to qualify for everything He is offering. 99.9% of God's promises are conditional. You will continually find God saying, "If you will do X, then I will do Y." Again, we aren't talking about a works based theology; but a faith based theology that requires us to submit to His authority and leading.

Another example of this is found in Deuteronomy 11:18-23 where God declares, "[18] "Therefore you shall lay up these words of mine in your heart and in your soul, and bind them as a sign on your hand, and they shall be as frontlets between your eyes. [19] You shall teach them to your children, speaking of them when you sit in your house, when you walk by the way, when you lie down, and when you rise up. [20] And you shall write them on the doorposts of your house and on your gates, [21] that your days and the days of your children may be multiplied in the land of which the LORD swore to your fathers to give them, like the days of the heavens above the earth. [22] *"For if you carefully keep all these commandments* which I command you to do—to love the LORD your God, to walk in all His ways, and to hold fast to Him— [23] *then the LORD will* drive out all these nations from before you, and you will dispossess greater and mightier nations than yourselves." (Emphasis Added).

What are the conditions to receiving God's promise? He said that we had to hide His Word in our hearts, teach His Word to our children, speak His Word, and make His Word the centerpiece of our lives by keeping His commands. Then He would give us and our children a lengthy life. Then He would defeat your enemies. And then He would Bless us and give us our enemy's lands.

That reminds me of Deuteronomy 6:4-12, "[4] "Hear, O Israel: The LORD our God, the LORD is one! [5] You shall love the LORD your God with all your heart, with all your soul, and with all your strength. [6] "And these words which I command you today shall be in your heart. [7] You shall teach them diligently to your children, and shall talk of them when you sit in your house, when you walk by the way, when you lie down, and when you rise up. [8] You shall bind them as a sign on your hand, and they shall be as frontlets between your eyes. [9] You shall write them on the doorposts of your house and on your gates. [10] "So it shall be, when the LORD your God brings you into the land of which He swore to your fathers, to Abraham, Isaac, and Jacob, to give you large and beautiful cities which you did not build, [11] houses full of all good things, which you did not fill, hewn-out wells which you did not dig, vineyards and olive trees which you did not plant—when you have eaten and are full— [12] then beware, lest you forget the LORD who brought you out of the land of Egypt, from the house of bondage."

Even though this is part of the Old Covenant, we still have access to these promises because Jesus said He didn't come to destroy the Law (the Old Covenant), but to fulfill it. The Good News is that along with these promises we also have access to even better promises in a New and Better Covenant established IN Jesus.

In Matthew 5:17-18 Jesus declares, "[17] "Do not think that I came to destroy the Law or the Prophets [the Old Testament truths]. I did not come to destroy but to fulfill. [18] For assuredly, I say to you, till heaven and earth pass away, one jot or one tittle will by no means pass from the law till all is fulfilled." Jesus is the reason we have access to the Blessing. He is the mediator of the Blessing. He gave us access to a BETTER COVENANT OF PROMISES and opportunities our ancestors never had access to, because the price for sin hadn't been paid for yet.

Hebrews 7:22 says, "By so much more Jesus has become a surety of a better covenant."

Hebrews 8:6-7 tells us, "⁶ But now He has obtained a more excellent ministry, inasmuch as He is also Mediator of a better covenant, which was established on better promises. ⁷ For if that first covenant had been faultless, then no place would have been sought for a second."

Hebrews 12:22-24 declares, "²² But you have come to Mount Zion and to the city of the living God, the heavenly Jerusalem, to an innumerable company of angels, ²³ to the general assembly and church of the firstborn who are registered in heaven, to God the Judge of all, to the spirits of just men made perfect, ²⁴ to Jesus the Mediator of the new covenant, and to the blood of sprinkling that speaks better things than that of Abel."

What do all of those Scriptures mean? They mean that we are no longer slaves to a law which we cannot keep. Sin has penetrated this world to the core. These passages don't give us the right to continue in blatant sin and disregard for God's rules, but they do free us to understand and receive the grace of our loving God. You and I are free to live, free to ask for forgiveness when we blow it, free to receive mercy when we don't deserve it, and free to experience EVERY BLESSING that Jesus experiences as a sinless and perfect man. His substitutional death on the cross has freed us from the death we deserve.

Through Jesus death on the cross, you and I have gained access to all that Adam experienced before the fall. We've gained access to the throne room of God where all of His mercy resides. We are no longer separated by our sin. The sin debt has been paid in full, once and for all, by Jesus. We've become heirs to all God originally wanted us to have—WE ARE HEIRS to THE BLESSING!

Look at Romans 8:17 which says, "[16] The Spirit Himself bears witness with our spirit that we are children of God, [17] and if children, then heirs—heirs of God and joint heirs with Christ, if indeed we suffer with Him, that we may also be glorified together."

What does it mean to be an heir? It means we have an inheritance! It means that we have received something that originally belonged to somebody else—but has now been gifted to us. WE'RE RICH IN EVERY POSSIBLE WAY IMAGINABLE, and in ways we haven't the slightest clue about yet.

There is so much that God wants to give us, but sin and an incorrect understanding of the Bible has kept many of us from receiving all that God has made available to us IN JESUS. People have been taught that suffering and lack are part and parcel with holiness—but that couldn't be any further from the truth! That is not Bible—in fact, that is demonic deception. There is not one thing we can ever add to the complete salvation we have when we receive Jesus as our personal Lord and Savior. He has paid the full price necessary for us to experience wholeness in every area of our lives. I don't care if you became the next Mother Teresa, or if you lived like one of the Desert Fathers from the Early Church—denying yourself of basic needs. That would still never make you one ounce more forgiven or accepted than you are now—you'd just be suffering unnecessarily. It was Jesus' suffering and death on the cross that has restored you to your Heavenly Father.

Don't be deceived by Satan's tactics—you are no more or less saved now than you were the moment you received Jesus as Lord. The only difference between a baby Christian and a person who has been saved for years, is the time that person has had to grow in maturity. The more time an individual has spent with the Lord, the more he or she should be bearing fruit and growing in relationship to Him and His Word.

Being Blessed is not something to be ashamed of—in fact, the Blessing is part of our spiritual heritage in Jesus. We've been given everything we could ever need or desire IN HIM. We've been given access to perfect health; we've received the ability to enjoy life and live in PEACE, security, and soundness of mind and spirit. Jesus has made available to us perfect protection, great relationships, Godly and obedient children, and yes, even FINANCIAL WEALTH!

Uh Oh, this preacher is talking about money—string him up quick! No! God knows what your needs are even before you do. He's not opposed to giving you those things if your heart is focused on Him and His Word. He knows His sheep—those who are Kingdom minded, those He can trust to use the things He Blesses them with to do His will. God wants His people to enjoy the BLESSING which He has commanded upon them.

God explains to us what THE BLESSING is, so that even a theologian can't confuse us about it! If we study this passage we will find that there is nothing we could ever desire, that has been omitted from The Blessing of God!

Deuteronomy 28:1-14 says, *"Now it shall come to pass, if you diligently obey the voice of the LORD your God*, to observe carefully all His commandments which I command you today, *that the LORD your God will set you high above all nations of the earth. ² And all these blessings shall come upon you and OVERTAKE YOU*, because you obey the voice of the LORD your God: ³ "**Blessed** shall you be in the city, and **blessed** shall you be in the country. ⁴ "**Blessed** shall be the fruit of your body, the produce of your ground and the increase of your herds, the increase of your cattle and the offspring of your flocks. ⁵ "**Blessed** shall be your basket and your kneading bowl. ⁶ "**Blessed** shall you be when you come in, **and blessed** shall you be when you go out. ⁷ "The LORD will cause your enemies who rise against you to be defeated before your face; they shall come out against you one way and flee before you seven ways. ⁸ *"The LORD will command the blessing on you in your storehouses and in all to which you set your hand, and He will bless you in the land which* *the LORD your God is giving you.* [9] "The LORD will establish you as a holy people to Himself, just as He has sworn to you*, if you* keep the commandments of the LORD your God and walk in His ways. [10] Then all peoples of the earth shall see that you are called by the name of the LORD, and they shall be afraid of you. [11] *And the LORD will grant you plenty of goods, in the fruit of your body, in the increase of your livestock, and in the produce of your ground*, in the land of which the LORD swore to your fathers to give you. [12] *The LORD will open to you His good treasure, the heavens, to give the rain to your land in its season, and to bless all the work of your hand. You shall lend to many nations, but you shall not borrow.* [13] And *the LORD will make you the head and not the tail; you shall be above only, and not be beneath*, *if* you heed the commandments of the LORD your God, which I command you today, and are careful to observe them. [14] So you shall not turn aside from any of the words which I command you this day, to the right or the left, to go after other gods to serve them." (Emphasis Added).

Proverbs 10:22 sums up the reason for the Blessing, *"The blessing of the LORD makes one rich, and He adds no sorrow with it."* (Emphasis Added). The Blessing will make you rich in friends, rich in family, rich in health, rich in relationship with God, rich in finances, and rich in every other area of your life. You are rich because you are BLESSED IN CHRIST JESUS. You definitely have something to shout about!!! Praise God!!

Daily Declaration

I declare that I am BLESSED, Highly Favored, and Empowered to prosper in every area of my life. God has commanded His BLESSING upon me. He has promised that **IF I OBEY HIM**, His BLESSING will come upon me and overtake me. I receive it now in Jesus name. I commit myself to Him eternally. I refuse to allow the Devil, religious thinking, or denominational traditions to cheat me out of the BLESSING which God has made available to me IN JESUS. If God didn't want me to be prosperous—then He would have never promised prosperity to me in the Bible. I am completely convinced that as a joint-heir IN CHRIST, I am supposed to enjoy a higher standard of living than the World enjoys. I declare by faith that no recession, no economic downturn, and no demon in Hell can keep me from the plan of God for my life. I declare that I AM a Blessing magnet! I AM a love magnet and I distribute and exude love to everyone I come in contact with! I AM a magnet attracting PERFECT HEALTH and WHOLENESS to my body! I AM a magnet to God's SUPERNATURAL FAVOR and GRACE! And I AM a PROSPERITY MAGNET and I live in the ABUNDANCE and OVERFLOW of God's AMAZING LOVE! Nothing can separate me from God. He has BLESSED me so that I can be a BLESSING to others. I have made up my mind and I will receive and distribute His BLESSING to all who encounter me, in Jesus' name, AMEN!

Day 20
The Law Of Giving And Receiving

"[15] Now you Philippians know also that in the beginning of the gospel, when I departed from Macedonia, no church shared with me concerning giving and receiving but you only. [16] For even in Thessalonica you sent aid once and again for my necessities. [17] *Not that I seek the gift, but I seek the fruit that abounds to your account.*"

Philippians 4:15-17 (NKJV, Emphasis Added)

Many Christians have spent years giving into the ministry of the Gospel. They have been faithful tithers who have sown of their finances obediently and given cheerfully, but have become frustrated because they have not fully experienced the promises found in the Bible.

In Malachi 3:10-12 God instructs us to, "Bring all the tithes into the storehouse, that there may be food in My house, and try Me now in this," says the LORD of hosts, "If I will not open for you the windows of heaven and pour out for you such blessing that there will not be room enough to receive it. [11] "And I will rebuke the devourer for your sakes, so that he will not destroy the fruit of your ground, nor shall the vine fail to bear fruit for you in the field," says the LORD of hosts; [12] "And all nations will call you blessed, for you will be a delightful land," says the LORD of hosts."

Let me ask you a question. How many of you have received so much that there is not enough room to receive more? I would venture to guess not many! This world is filled with people who are continually trying to get more—wouldn't you agree?

We've got to remember however, that our personal experience does not make the Word of God void. The Bible teaches us that God's Word is the greatest guarantee of all. In Hebrews 6:13-14 we read, "[13] For when God made a promise to Abraham, because He could swear by no one greater, He swore by Himself, [14] saying, "Surely blessing I will bless you, and multiplying I will multiply you." God swore by Himself (by His name), because there was nothing greater than His name to swear by. His Word is a covenant promise.

Numbers 23:19 says, "God is not a man, that He should lie, nor a son of man, that He should repent. Has He said, and will He not do? Or has He spoken, and will He not make it good?"

Isaiah 55:11 declares, "So shall My word be that goes forth from My mouth; It shall not return to Me void, but it shall accomplish what I please, and it shall prosper in the thing for which I sent it."

Psalm 119:160 tells us, "The entirety of Your word is truth, and every one of Your righteous judgments endures forever."

John 17:17 states, "Sanctify them by Your truth. Your word is truth."

Hebrews 10:23 instructs, "Let us hold fast the confession of our hope without wavering, for He who promised is faithful."

And Titus 1:2 illustrates how trustworthy God's Word is by saying—He cannot lie, "In hope of eternal life which God, who cannot lie, promised before time began"

If these Scriptures are true, then how is it that many people fail to receive the manifestation of God's Word in their lives? I would venture to say it's because they have only understood part of this Biblical Law. They have understood that the Bible teaches us to sow our seeds, but they haven't matured in their faith to receive a harvest in return. They have been taught, and in some cases conned and manipulated, into giving until it hurts.

Instead of sowing into, they have "caved in" to the pleas of greedy charlatans who beg for money so that they live lavish lifestyles at the expense of the poor. Hoping to shut these con artists up and to rid themselves of the pressure to give—they empty their wallets or purses into the offering bucket.

I'm going to be blunt! I NEVER give to ministers who beg or put pressure on people. PEOPLE AREN'T THEIR SOURCE—GOD IS! Any minister who doesn't know that *shouldn't be in the ministry*. **God will provide when FAITH is applied!**

When people feel pressured to give they aren't giving the way they have been instructed to give—cheerfully and in faith. 2 Corinthians 9:7-8 (AMP) says, "[7]Let each one [give] as he has made up his own mind and purposed in his heart, not reluctantly or sorrowfully or under compulsion, for God loves (He takes pleasure in, prizes above other things, and is unwilling to abandon or to do without) a cheerful (joyous, "prompt to do it") giver [whose heart is in his giving]. [8]And God is able to make all grace (every favor and earthly blessing) come to you in abundance, so that you may always and under all circumstances and whatever the need be self-sufficient [possessing enough to require no aid or support and furnished in abundance for every good work and charitable donation]."

We are instructed to give as we are led by the Holy Spirit to give—as we have made up our mind, after praying, and asking God to instruct us where He wants us to sow HIS SEED. This is vitally important if we want to receive a harvest. We aren't supposed to throw our tithes and offerings into the bucket as it passes; we are to WORSHIP GOD with our tithe—in EXPECTATION of RECEIVING **ALL** of our needs being met by God.

I'm not saying that we give only to receive. God is not the big slot machine in the sky. But His Word is Good! His Promises are true! And He has instructed us to believe Him for a return! It is the Law of Seedtime and Harvest found in Genesis 8:22, which dictates when we sow we will reap a harvest.

When a farmer plants corn, he does it expecting to receive a harvest of corn at harvest time. In fact, he expects to receive hundreds of times more corn than he originally planted. He expects to enjoy the fruit of his labor by eating some, selling some, and then having some left over to sow the next season.

In Mark 4:1-8 we find Jesus teaching this principle to His followers, "[1]AGAIN JESUS began to teach beside the lake. And a very great crowd gathered about Him, so that He got into a ship in order to sit in it on the sea, and the whole crowd was at the lakeside on the shore. [2]And He taught them many things in parables (illustrations or comparisons put beside truths to explain them), and in His teaching He said to them: [3]Give attention to this! Behold, a sower went out to sow. [4]And as he was sowing, some seed fell along the path, and the birds came and ate it up. [5]Other seed [of the same kind] fell on ground full of rocks, where it had not much soil; and at once it sprang up, because it had no depth of soil; [6]And when the sun came up, it was scorched, and because it had not taken root, it withered away. [7]Other

seed [of the same kind] fell among thorn plants, and the thistles grew and pressed together and utterly choked and suffocated it, and it yielded no grain. [8]And other seed [of the same kind] fell into good (well-adapted) soil and brought forth grain, growing up and increasing, and yielded up to thirty times as much, and sixty times as much, and even a hundred times as much as had been sown."

In verse 13 Jesus took it a step further by saying that sowing and reaping was the foundation to everything that we can learn in the Bible. He asked His disciples, "Do you not understand this parable? How then will you understand all the parables?" In other words Jesus was saying to them, "This is how the entire Kingdom of God operates—everything begins by planting a seed and expecting a harvest."

Remember in Matthew 17:20, Jesus said, "…for assuredly, I say to you, if you have faith as a mustard seed…" faith is a precious seed that we must plant into our spirit believing God for our harvest. The Apostle Paul called Jesus the Head or the original Seed which was sown for all mankind. Paul compares Jesus and the Church to a seed which is continuing to grow and produce fruit. In Colossians 2:19 we read, "[Jesus] from whom all the body, *[is] nourished and knit together* by joints and ligaments, *grows with the increase that is from God.*" [Emphasis Added]. In fact Jesus is called the seed of woman in Genesis 3:14 and Galatians 4:4. He is called the Seed of David in 2 Samuel 7:12-14, and Romans 1:3-4. He is referred to as the Seed of Abraham in Genesis 22:18 and Galatians 3:16. And the Bible calls Him the first-fruit or first born of many brethren in Romans 8:29. Jesus was born as a man, He died on the Cross of Calvary, and sown as the Father's seed in order that He could enjoy a harvest of Believers who were washed clean of sin and made righteous IN JESUS.

2 Corinthians 5:17-21 says it this way, "[17] Therefore, if anyone is in Christ, he is a new creation; old things have passed away; behold, all things have become new. [18] Now all things are of God, who has reconciled us to Himself through Jesus Christ, and has given us the ministry of reconciliation, [19] that is, that God was in Christ reconciling the world to Himself, not imputing their trespasses to them, and has committed to us the word of reconciliation. [20] Now then, we are ambassadors for Christ, as though God were pleading through us: we implore you on Christ's behalf, be reconciled to God. [21] For He made Him who knew no sin to be sin for us, that we might become the righteousness of God in Him."

Jesus didn't only tell us that we need to sow, but He also taught us to be cognizant of the soil we are sowing into because the soil can help determine our yield. In the Bible the soil represents our spirit and the quality of our faith. We must not only have the faith to give, but also to receive a harvest on the seeds we have sown.

In Philippians 4:15, Paul tells the Philippians, "...No church shared with me concerning giving and receiving but you only." He said, GIVING and RECEIVING, NOT JUST GIVING! Yes, we are supposed to give into ministry because we love God and are thankful for His provision in our lives. But we are also expected to have the faith to receive our provision back from God. Hebrews 11:6 (AMP) says, "But without faith it is impossible to please and be satisfactory to Him. For whoever would come near to God must [necessarily] believe that God exists and that He is the rewarder of those who earnestly and diligently seek Him [out]." In other words, God rewards expectant faith. He rewards those who know that He is a loving and giving God.

John 3:16 exemplifies this truth by saying, "For God so loved the world that He gave [Jesus]..."

Jesus knows how hard it can be for some to let go of a thing that they deem as being "their" precious seed. In Mark 10:23-31 He taught His disciples saying, "[23] How hard it is for those who have riches to enter the kingdom of God!" [24] And the disciples were astonished at His words. But Jesus answered again and said to them, "Children, how hard it is for those who trust in riches to enter the kingdom of God! [25] It is easier for a camel to go through the eye of a needle than for a rich man to enter the kingdom of God." [26] And they were greatly astonished, saying among themselves, "Who then can be saved?" [27] But Jesus looked at them and said, "With men *it is* impossible, but not with God; for with God all things are possible." [28] Then Peter began to say to Him, "See, we have left all and followed You." [29] So Jesus answered and said, "Assuredly, I say to you, there is no one who has left house or brothers or sisters or father or mother or wife or children or lands, for My sake and the gospel's, [30] who shall not receive a hundredfold now in this time—houses and brothers and sisters and mothers and children and lands, with persecutions—and in the age to come, eternal life. [31] But many who are first will be last, and the last first."

Jesus had just finished speaking to the rich young ruler and had told him in verses 21-22, "One thing you lack: Go your way, sell whatever you have and give to the poor, and you will have treasure in heaven; and come, take up the cross, and follow Me." ²² But he was sad at this word, and went away sorrowful, for he had great possessions."

Jesus wasn't asking this man to make a vow of poverty. He wasn't saying, "If you want to be 'Holy' like me you can't ever own anything nice." That is such "religious" thinking! Jesus knew this man's heart. He knew that the man didn't just own material things, but that those material things owned him! Jesus also knew that this man could not devote himself fully to the task of loving and serving others if his focus was on his personal "stuff" instead of the desire to see other people living a Blessed life.

Many Christians are the same way. They hold onto things so tightly fearing that if they don't, they won't have enough for the things they want for themselves. They fear that if they go All-in God will take what they have and they will be without. But God wants us to enjoy our wealth. He wants us to enjoy material things along with spiritual things, but He doesn't want those things to take away from the most important things in life—Loving God and loving others. (See Deuteronomy 6:5 and Matthew 22:37-40.

In order to live successfully we must have a correct understanding of money and the tithe. Leviticus 27:30 declares, "And all the tithe... is the LORD's. It is holy to the LORD." The tithe is only 10% of our income. What you do with the other 90% is up to you. God wants you to enjoy your money, enjoy your stuff, and to enjoy your life, but He doesn't want those things to own you like they did the Rich Young Ruler.

Money is neither good nor bad—it is neutral! Money is a tool that we use in this natural world. Jesus came and died on the cross to set us free from sin, sickness, poverty, lack, and everything else that is associated with the Curse.

2 Corinthians 8:9 declares, "For you know the grace of our Lord Jesus Christ, that though He was rich, yet for your sakes He became poor, that you through His poverty might become rich."

God needs people who are in covenant relationship with Him to fund His work. He doesn't have a problem with you having and enjoying money. He understands that if He gives it to you, you will take a portion of it to Bless His work in reaching people with the Gospel of Jesus Christ.

The problem is that even though God is trying to Bless us we are often failing at receiving the harvest He has intended for us to have. Many of us haven't been believing to receive our harvest once we have sown our seeds We have been convinced by society and ultimately by Satan, that money is evil, unholy, and only for those who are greedy. We have also been conned into believing that if we give to God He may withhold what we need—that we cannot count on His faithfulness when it comes to our finances or anything else. But Luke 6:38 (ERV) promises us, "Give to others, and you will receive. You will be given much. It will be poured into your hands—more than you can hold. You will be given so much that it will spill into your lap. The way you give to others is the way God will give to you."

I encourage you to be bold and to trust God—His Word never fails! Sow your seeds in faith today believing for YOUR harvest to come back to you in such abundance that you can't possible receive it all in.

God wants and needs covenant partners who will support His ministry work of delivering the Gospel message to the world. When we accomplish God's vision we will do as Reinhard Bonnke says and, "Make Heaven full and Hell empty!" Praise God! Make it a point to find a good Word church and to sow into them today! Step out in faith believing God for the impossible! Mark 9:23 says, "If you can believe, all things are possible to him who believes." Believe, Sow, and RECEIVE to the glory of God in Jesus!

Daily Declaration

I declare that I am a doer of the Word! I am a sower and I sow my seed in faith believing for my harvest. I trust that God has my best interests at heart. I believe that He loves me and will never allow me to go without. Psalm 37:25-26 says of me, "I have been young, and now am old; yet I have not seen the righteous forsaken, nor his descendants begging bread. [26] He is ever merciful, and lends; and his descendants are blessed." I declare the Blessing is mine! God has so highly Blessed and Favored me and my family because He has spoken His Blessing over me. I laugh at fear and command it to flee far from me. I chuckle at worry and doubt saying to them, "My God is BIG, and He Loves me!" Like David I declare to them "Pushed to the wall, I called to GOD; from the wide open spaces, He answered. GOD's now at my side and I'm not afraid; who would dare lay a hand on me? GOD's my strong champion; I flick off my enemies like flies. [It's] far better to take refuge in GOD than trust in people; far better to take refuge in GOD than trust in celebrities." (See Psalm 118:5-9, MSG). I am not moved by fear of lack, and I am not moved by whispers of my   destruction. I know that God is my Source. He is My Covenant keeping God, Who will never leave me or forsake me. I am only moved by my faith in His Word—and His faithfulness to surround me with His Blessing! (See Psalm 5:12). I pray all of this in Jesus' mighty name, Amen.

Day 21
God Is The Author Of Peace

"For God is not the author of confusion but of peace, as in all the churches of the saints."

1 Corinthians 14:33 (NKJV)

Anytime we encounter confusion we must immediately begin to understand what is taking place. The enemy is trying to utilize one of his tactics to draw us out of our perfect peace in Christ and out of the will of God for our lives. Confusion, like fear, creates uneasy feelings which move us from a position of confidence in God's love for us and peace (soundness within our spirit), into a position of fear, irritability, and anger. But we are told in 2 Timothy 1:7, "God has not given us a spirit of fear, but of power and of love and of a sound mind." Anything that is outside of complete confidence in His love for us and outside of operating by the fruit of the Spirit is not from God.

Ephesians 5:8-10 explains, "[8] For you were once darkness, but now you are light in the Lord. Walk as children of light [9] (for the fruit of the Spirit is in all goodness, righteousness, and truth), [10] finding out what is acceptable to the Lord."

We must understand that our God is a good God and the Devil is a bad devil. Everything good comes from our Heavenly Father and everything bad comes from Satan and from his twisting of God's Word and Character—which can only produce the Curse.

Galatians 5:22-23 (NLT) lists the fruit of the Spirit, "[22] But the Holy Spirit produces this kind of fruit in our lives: love, joy, peace, patience, kindness, goodness, faithfulness, [23] gentleness, and self-control. There is no law against these things!"

Every one of these characteristics is an attribute of Love Himself—an attribute of God. When we are patient with others, we are others focused. When we are gentle, we are considerate and careful of others feelings. When we are joyful, we are content in our circumstances knowing that even in trials, God will help us to overcome evil and move us back over into His perfect peace and wholeness.

God's plan for our lives is order; it is not a chaotic mess! Chaos causes anxiety, stress, and even strife. 1 Corinthians 14:40 instructs us to, "Let all things be done decently and in order." Why? Because when all things are carried out in order there is no room for confusion and division. Clear understanding leads to faith and actions which ultimately lead to LOVE.

Confusion is a weapon the enemy uses to try to steal the peace we receive from the promises in the Bible. If Satan can cause confusion, if he can keep us from understanding the truth of the Word, he can manipulate what we believe, and ultimately, our destination. But in order for him to accomplish his devious task—he has to have your permission. He has to convince you to give up. He must cause you to become confused about what the Bible says, and cause you to have an incorrect perception of who you are IN CHRIST!

In Matthew 13:11-15 Jesus said, "It has been given to you to know the mysteries of the kingdom of heaven, but to them it has not been given [to those who have rejected Jesus]. [12] For whoever has, to him more will be given, and he will have abundance; but whoever does not have, even what he has will be taken away from him. [13] Therefore I speak to them in parables, because seeing they do not see, and hearing they do not hear, nor do they understand. [14] And in them the prophecy of Isaiah is fulfilled, which says: 'Hearing you will hear and shall not understand, and seeing you will see and not perceive; [15] For the hearts of this people have grown dull [irreverent, and lacking interest]. Their ears are hard of hearing, and their eyes they have closed, lest they should see with their eyes and hear with their ears, lest they should understand with their hearts and turn, so that I should heal them.'"

Jesus is saying that when confusion and lack of understanding are combined people can hear and see the truth but still reject it. That is exactly what Satan desires—if we don't understand who we are or what we have access to IN CHRIST, we are powerless against sin and the enemy's lies.

In Matthew 13:18 Jesus says, "Therefore hear the parable of the sower: [19] When anyone hears the word of the Kingdom, and does not understand it, then the wicked one [Satan] comes and snatches away what was sown in his heart."

The devil is a thief! We know that from John 10:10 (AMP), "The thief comes only in order to steal and kill and destroy. I came that they may have and enjoy life, and have it in abundance (to the full, till it overflows)." Satan comes to steal the Word [the Biblical promises made to us by God which tell us what belongs to us because of Jesus].

Moreover, God wants us to enjoy life! He wants us to understand all that has been made available to us as heirs to His promises (See Galatians 3:29). But in order to do so, we have to learn to press into the Word and then keep pressing until what the Bible promises has manifested in our live. It's a combination of understanding God's Word in combination with persistence in faith that drives confusion completely out of our lives. Faith believes regardless of current circumstances. Faith always puts pressure on the Word until that Word changes our present environment to match God's promises.

When we learn the truth behind confusion and when we learn how to get rid of it by continuing to walk by faith and not by sight (See 2 Corinthians 5:7), then we are able to cast out fear, anxiety, confusion, and doubt. It is then that we move into the Fruit of the Spirit which is—Love, Joy, Peace, Patience, Kindness, Goodness, Faithfulness, Gentleness, and Self-Control. (Galatians 5:22-23).

Philippians 4:6-8 commands us, "⁶ Be anxious for nothing, but in everything by prayer and supplication, with thanksgiving, let your requests be made known to God; ⁷ *and the peace of God*, which surpasses all understanding, will guard your hearts and minds through Christ Jesus. ⁸ Finally, brethren, whatever things are true, whatever things are noble, whatever things are just, whatever things are pure, whatever things are lovely, whatever things are of good report, if there is any virtue and if there is anything praiseworthy— meditate on these things." (Emphasis Added). Peace is the byproduct of a spirit which is established on God and His Word!

When you meditate on a thing, it is like chewing on it until every bit of that *thing's* essence has come out of it. A good comparison would be like chewing on a piece of gum until all of the flavor has been chewed out of it. Another definition of meditation is to mutter or to speak a thing over and over. We can choose to either meditate positively or negatively. Negative meditation is fear or worry. Positive meditation is faith. When we obey Philippians 4:8 and meditate only on those things which are true, noble, lovely and of a good report—it builds faith and peace on the inside of us. But when we meditate on negative things, it creates fear, worry, doubt, and confusion on the inside of our spirit.

Remember, God is not the author of confusion. He is the author of peace. In fact, Jesus is known as the Prince of Peace (See Isaiah 9:6). God has given us His Word (the Bible), which is His will for our lives. God is not trying to hide His will from us; He is trying to get it to us, so that we can defeat Satan in every battle.

Ephesians 5:17 encourages us, "Therefore do not be unwise, but understand what the will of the Lord is." It is Satan who is trying to confuse and to steal the plan of God from us. He wants us to become fearful and powerless against his attacks. Don't allow confusion to attach its ugly self to you. Instead search out the will of God in the Scriptures and find the Peace of God which surpasses all understanding—and Begin Living Your Victorious Life In Jesus Christ today!

Daily Declaration

I declare that I live and operate in the PERFECT PEACE of God! I have not been given the spirit of fear but of Love, Power, and a Sound mind! Jesus told me in John 14:27, "Peace I leave with you, My peace I give to you; not as the world gives do I give to you. Let not your heart be troubled, neither let it be afraid." *Eirene*, is the Greek word which is translated peace in the English. Strong's Concordance and Thayer's Greek Lexicon define *eirene*, as being peace, security, safety, and prosperity. Thayer's goes further by saying that *eirene*, is the tranquil state of peace which leads to salvation. I declare that I receive the peace that Jesus has provided for me. Jesus has given me WHOLENESS in every area of my life! I'm Blessed! I'm Prosperous! I'm Safe and Secure! And I lack NOTHING IN CHRIST! Thank You Jesus for giving me everything I could ever possibly need or desire. Not only have You given me Salvation in the sense that I will spend eternity with You, but You have given me Salvation in the sense of total life prosperity and wholeness! I have NOTHING to fear because You are my Lord! I speak PEACE over my family. I speak PEACE over my finances and my career. And I speak PEACE over my body, my mind, will, and emotion, and over my health. I pray all of these things in Jesus' name, Amen.

Day 22
I Think Myself Happy

"¹Then Agrippa said to Paul, "You are permitted to speak for yourself." So Paul stretched out his hand and answered for himself: ² "I think myself happy, King Agrippa, because today I shall answer for myself before you concerning all the things of which I am accused by the Jews, ³ especially because you are expert in all customs and questions which have to do with the Jews. Therefore I beg you to hear me patiently."

Acts 26:1-3 (NKJV)

Did you know that happiness and joy are not the same? Joy is based on what you know to be true about God, His character, and His Word, while happiness is based on a person's emotions and is   determined by their feelings about their current circumstances.

Nehemiah 8:10 tells us that the joy of the LORD is our strength. When we go through tough times, when trials occur in our lives, we rest in our faith knowing that God will deliver us out of them all.

Psalm 34:17-19 tells us, "¹⁷ The righteous cry out, *and the LORD hears, and delivers them out of all their troubles*. ¹⁸ The LORD is near to those who have a broken heart, and saves such as have a contrite spirit. ¹⁹ *Many are the afflictions of the righteous, but the LORD delivers him out of them all*." (Emphasis Added).

If we were to look at all our troubles from a purely natural perspective we might become unhappy, depressed, and want to give up. But, we can have joy in spite of them because we know that God is greater than our troubles and He will rescue us out of them all!

In Proverbs 23:7 we learn an amazing truth about ourselves, "For as he thinks in his heart, so is he…" The way that you and I think about our circumstances, our abilities, and our opportunities, determines whether or not we experience positive or negative results. We have the ability to choose how we think, and our choices show the world what we really believe about God and His will for our lives.

Dr. Caroline Leaf, a neuroscientist, writes in her book, *Who Switched Off My Brain? Controlling Toxic Thoughts and Emotions*, "A thought may seem harmless, but if it becomes toxic, even just a thought can become physically, emotionally or spiritually dangerous. Thoughts are measureable and occupy mental 'real estate.' Thoughts are active; they grow and change. Thoughts influence every decision, word, action, and physical reaction we make. Every time you have a thought, it is actively changing your brain and your body – for better or worse."

Leaf continues, "A massive body of research collectively shows that up to 80% of physical, emotional and mental health issues today could be a direct result of our thought lives."

Dr. Daniel G. Amen, a medical doctor writes in his book, *Change Your Brain, Change Your Life*, "Most people do not understand how important thoughts are and leave the development of thought patterns to chance. Did you know that every thought you have sends electrical signals throughout your brain? Thoughts have actual physical properties. They are real! They have significant influence on every cell in your body. When your mind is burdened with many negative thoughts, it affects your deep limbic system and causes deep limbic problems (irritability, moodiness, depression, etc.). Teaching yourself to control and direct your thoughts in a positive way is one of the most effective ways to feel better."

Our thoughts not only affect our attitudes, but science has proven that our thoughts release chemicals within our brains which actually change the neurons and create a sort of mental root system similar to tree roots or branches, which create patterns of behavior.

Dr. Leaf claims, "The surprising truth is that every single thought – whether it is positive or negative – goes through the same cycle when it forms. Thoughts are basically electrical impulses, chemicals and neurons. They look like a tree with branches. As the thoughts grow and become permanent, more branches grow and the connections become stronger. As we change our thinking, some of the branches go away, new ones form, the strength of the connections change, and the memories network with other thoughts. What an incredible capacity of the brain to change and rewire and grow! Spiritually, this is the renewing of the mind."

Leaf says, "As you think, your thoughts are activated, which in turn activates your attitude, because your attitude is all of your thoughts put together and reflects your state of mind. This attitude is reflected in the chemical secretions that are released. Positive attitudes cause secretion of the correct amount of chemicals, and negative attitudes distort the chemical secretions in a way that disrupts their natural flow. *The chemicals are like little cellular signals that translate the information of your thought into a physical reality in your body and mind, creating an emotion. The combination of thoughts, emotions, and resulting attitudes, impacts your body in a positive or negative way*. This means that your mind and body really are   inherently linked, and this link starts with your thoughts." (Emphasis Added).

2 Corinthians 10:4-6 (KJV), declares, "[4] For the weapons of our warfare are not carnal, but mighty through God to the pulling down of strong holds; [5] *Casting down imaginations*, and every high thing that exalteth itself against the knowledge of God, and bringing into captivity every thought to the obedience of Christ; [6] And having in a readiness to revenge all disobedience, when your obedience is fulfilled." (Emphasis Added).

Do you see that? We are to cast down or eradicate our mind of negative thoughts and images which those imaginations and their originator—Satan, try to get us to focus on. As Believers, we have been given the authority to change our thoughts. We have been given the power to determine what we will allow to occupy the real estate of our minds and what we will cast out—the choice is up to us.

The most frequent attack the enemy uses is to suggest negative and fearful thoughts. He does not have the ability to read our minds but he can tell if his tactics are working based on how we respond. His goal is to take our attention away from the promises of God.

He is constantly prowling around to see his assault is working. He listens to the words we are speaking and he watches the actions we take once those negative thoughts have been deployed in our minds. What we do and say illustrates to him whether or not he's winning.

In Acts 26, we find Paul on trial before King Agrippa. His life and the Gospel of Jesus have been brought up on false charges and accusations. But instead of automatically thinking the worst, instead of giving up and caving in to fear and all of the negative circumstances he faced, instead of feeling sorry for himself, Paul says something amazing that we all need to take notice of. He says, "I think myself happy, King Agrippa…"

Paul is not just talking about being happy in the sense that everything is hunky-dory! He is saying that even in the midst of fighting for his life he still is able to have joy because of the knowledge he has about his God. He knows that even in uncomfortable situations, God is faithful! He knows that God is willing and capable of delivering him out of **ALL** his troubles—including this one! He's learned to cast down every imagination and every thought that tries to exalt itself above the truth of God's faithfulness to deliver him. And He refuses to allow any negative thoughts to occupy space in his mind because he knows how destructive those thoughts can be—AS A MAN THINKS SO IS HE!

But our battle isn't lost! In fact, we are more than conquerors IN CHRIST JESUS! I don't care what things look like in the natural realm—even when our lives are on the line and the devil is whispering in our ears how he has won the present battle. Even when the Devil has knit together a web of lies, trying to convince us that

148

there is no hope or conceivable way out of our present trial, we can still determine to stand firm before our faithful God. He will not leave us or forsake us—we have His Word on it!

We must become resolute in trusting the promises of God and believing Scriptures like Isaiah 54:17 which promises, "No weapon formed against you shall prosper, and every tongue which rises against you in judgment you shall condemn. This is the heritage of the servants of the LORD, and their righteousness is from Me," says the LORD."

The next time Satan does something to try to undermine your faith—what will you choose? Will you choose to fall for his deceptive tricks or will you make the conscious decision to THINK YOURSELF HAPPY?

Daily Declaration

I declare that my mind and my spirit are steadfastly fixed on the promises of God! I meditate and speak only those things that He has promised to me in His Word. Day and night I contemplate the things that God has said about me. I renew my mind to those promises and bring them to pass by faith. (See Joshua 1:8, 1 Corinthians 12:1-2). I constantly cast down the lies and false images that the enemy tries to feed into my subconscious mind. I rebuke the Devil and he flees from me in Jesus' name! And I think myself happy, I enjoy prosperity, and I have good success. (See Joshua 1:8, Acts 26:2). I am more than a conqueror in Christ! I am an Ambassador of Jesus with diplomatic immunity—untouchable by Satan and his cohorts (See Romans 8:37, 2 Corinthians 5:20). Thank You Jesus for saving me and for giving me Your mind and perfect peace. (See 1 Corinthians 2:16, John 14:27). I Bless you Lord, and thank You for all that You are doing in me, around me, and through me, and I pray all of these things in the mighty name of Jesus, Amen.

Day 23
You're Not In This Alone!

"¹⁶ At my first defense no one stood with me, but all forsook me. May it not be charged against them.¹⁷ But the Lord stood with me and strengthened me, so that the message might be preached fully through me, and that all the Gentiles might hear. Also I was delivered out of the mouth of the lion.¹⁸ And the Lord will deliver me from every evil work and preserve me for His heavenly kingdom. To Him be glory forever and ever. Amen!"

2 Timothy 4:16-18 (NKJV)

How many times have you felt like it was you against the world? Have you ever felt like you were never going to accomplish a task or goal that you had set out to do, or that if you did you'd have to do it all by yourself? Have you ever felt like everyone else was too wrapped up in their own stuff to give a hoot about you and your needs? I think we all have had moments when our flesh wanted to have its own pity party, but we are not ruled by our feelings or emotions. We are not moved by what we see or what we hear! We are only moved by our faith in the living Word of God! Hallelujah!

2 Corinthians 5:7 says, "For we walk by faith, not by sight." When we allow our emotions to govern our decisions, then faith always goes right out the window and we get ourselves into trouble.

It's important to understand that though we are social beings, though we were created to interact and live together, people don't complete us—God does! Anything that we lack from an emotional, physical, material, or spiritual perspective, we can only be made whole through our intimate relationship with Jesus. **HE IS OUR SOURCE FOR EVERYTHING!**

Your spouse can never totally fulfill all your needs and desires even if you are both born-again Believers and sensitive to the leading of the Holy Spirit and living out the Word together. There are some things that can only be obtained from God. We must come to the understanding that it is only through that threefold union that we are unstoppable and Victorious over the works of Satan!

Ecclesiastes 4:11-12 explains, "[11] Again, if two lie down together, they will keep warm; but how can one be warm alone? [12] Though one may be overpowered by another, two can withstand him. And a threefold cord is not quickly broken."

Anytime we begin to feel like it is us against the world. Any time the enemy tries to tell us that no one cares about us or that we're not significant; **IMMEDIATELY STOP AND REGROUP!** Cast down those false imaginations (2 Corinthians 10:5). STOP! the drama from going any further and remember that Proverbs 18:24 tells us that, "A man who has friends must himself be friendly, but there is a friend who sticks closer than a brother." Jesus, our Lord and Savior is that friend. He will never leave us or forsake us. He'll never leave us to fight our battles alone.

In other words, it all comes down to the law of seedtime and harvest. If we want to be loved, we must first sow our love to Jesus and to others. If we want the Lord to be our friend, we must first be friendly by inviting Him into our lives. We always reap what we sow. Even when we have sown love and friendship to others but are not yet seeing the fruit of those seeds manifested in our lives, we must remember that God is ALWAYS there!

He is the one who always sticks closer than a brother. And as Hebrews 13:5-6 promises us, "for He [God] Himself has said, I will not in any way fail you nor give you up nor leave you without support. [I will] not, I will] not, [I will] not in any degree leave you helpless nor forsake nor let [you] down (relax My hold on you)! [Assuredly not!] [6] So we take comfort and are encouraged and confidently and boldly say, The Lord is my Helper; I will not be seized with alarm [I will not fear or dread or be terrified]. What can man do to me?" You're Not In This Alone – God is right there with you to deliver you out of every circumstance you will ever face— Just call out His name and He will surely be there to see you through. JESUS IS LORD! AMEN!

Daily Declaration

I declare that God is for me! He is with me every step that I take, and He is my covenant partner who never leaves me nor forsakes me because He has vowed to be my God. Jeremiah 32:38-41 says to me, "[38] They shall be My people, and I will be their God; [39] then I will give them one heart and one way, that they may fear [worshipfully respect and revere] Me forever, for the good of them and their children after them. [40] And I will make an everlasting covenant with them, that I will not turn away from doing them good; but I will put My fear [worshipful respect] in their hearts so that they will not depart from Me. [41] Yes, I will rejoice over them to do them good, and I will assuredly plant them in this land, with all My heart and with all My soul." In Ezekiel 37:26-27 God has said, "[26] Moreover I will make a covenant of peace with them, and it shall be an everlasting covenant with them; I will establish them and multiply them, and I will set My sanctuary in their midst forevermore. [27] My tabernacle [My Holy Spirit] also shall be with them; indeed I will be their God, and they shall be My people." And finally, in 2 Corinthians 6:16 says, "[16] And what agreement has the temple of God with idols? For you are the temple of the living God. As God has said: "I will dwell in them and walk among them. I will be their God, and they shall be My people." Hallelujah! God is always with me! His Holy Spirit is living inside of me now because I have made Him My God and King. In fact, it was prophesied about Jesus in Matthew 1:23, "Behold, the virgin shall be with child, and bear a Son, *and they shall call His name Immanuel," which is translated, "God with us."* (Emphasis Added).

God is with me now in Jesus' name! I'm not alone and I will never be left alone or orphaned because my god loves me! Thank You Lord for Your comfort, Your Joy, and Your unmerited favor which always surrounds me like a shield (See Psalms 5:12). I am grateful for Your unfailing Love! I pray these things in Jesus' name, Amen.

Day 24
God's Not Mad At You—You Have Been Restored To Grace

"¹Therefore, having been justified by faith, we have peace with God through our Lord Jesus Christ, ² through whom also we have access by faith into this grace in which we stand, and rejoice in hope of the glory of God."

Romans 5:1-2 (NKJV)

So many people shy away from God and Christianity because they have been taught that God is mad at them! They have been convinced that they will never measure up to God's standard, so they think to themselves why should I even try. They have been told that their pasts exclude them from being able to experience God's best in their lives—*but **ALL** of those things aren't lies!*

It's true that we will never measure up on our own, but the good news is that we don't have to. Jesus has already justified us through the shedding of His blood on the cross! He has fully satisfied the penalty for our sins and has redeemed and justified us completely! He has completely satisfied and extinguished the wrath that God once had toward us because of our sins! There is nothing that we can do in order to earn our own salvation—but Jesus bought us back from death and restored us to life through His death on the Cross! We are FREE from the penalty of sin Hallelujah! Jesus has redeemed us with His Blood!

If we continue reading in Romans 5:8-11 we learn, "⁸ But God demonstrates His own love toward us, in that while we were still sinners, Christ died for us. ⁹ Much more then, having now been justified by His blood, we shall be saved from wrath through Him. ¹⁰ For if when we were enemies we were reconciled to God through the death of His Son, much more, having been reconciled, we shall be saved by His life. ¹¹ And not only that, but we also rejoice in God through our Lord Jesus Christ, through whom we have now received the reconciliation."

Do you see that? We are to rejoice in the fact that we have been reconciled to God. The sin that once separated us from His grace has been fully repaired and we've been restored—Praise God! There is no longer anything keeping us from interacting and receiving the promises of God, because of Jesus, our mediator of the New Covenant has restored us to the Father's grace/unmerited favor through the shedding of His blood. **The DEBT OF SIN has been PAID IN FULL!**

Isaiah 54:8-9 explains our relationship with God prior to Jesus' substitutional sacrifice for us. "⁸ With a little wrath I hid My face from you for a moment; but with everlasting kindness I will have mercy on you," says the LORD, your Redeemer. ⁹ "For this is like the waters of Noah to Me*; for as I have sworn that the waters of Noah would no longer cover the earth, so have I sworn that I would not be angry with you, nor rebuke you.*"

Healing has come to us for the sin which once separated us from God. Restitution and provision has been made for our sins which once blocked us from the Father's grace and covenant promises. Jesus has dealt with our sin problem and has eternally destroyed its power and authority over us once and for all.

Isaiah chapter 53 comes before chapter 54. In Isaiah 53 there is a prophetic declaration made by the prophet concerning the Messiah's arrival in the earth and His provision for salvation to all who would believe and receive the FREE GIFT. In Chapter 54 Isaiah describes the role that Christ came to fulfill as Messiah.

Just as God will never again flood the earth like He did during the days of Noah, we are told in Isaiah 54:9, that God swore He would never again be angry with those who were ***MADE RIGHTEOUS in His Son***—JESUS! All of His previous wrath because of our sin was placed on Jesus when He was nailed to the cross of Calvary. **PLEASE UNDERSTAND THAT <u>GOD IS NOT MAD AT YOU</u>!** And He isn't keeping anything from you—He has given you everything in the person of JESUS! Your only rational response would be to receive the free gift He is offering you and to repent for your sins. Receive your pardon! Receive His mercy! Receive His amazing grace and His unfailing love which are available to you now—IN JESUS!

Isaiah 43:25 declares, "I, even I, am He who blots out your transgressions for My own sake; and I will not remember your sins."

In Hebrews 8:12 God says, "[12] For I will be merciful to their unrighteousness, and their sins and their lawless deeds I will remember no more."

And finally, in Psalm 103:12 the psalmist declares, "As far as the east is from the west, so far has He removed our transgressions from us."

Stop allowing the devil to remind you of your past sins—Jesus has already dealt with them and has restored you to righteousness in Him. Sin no longer has authority over you if you have confessed Jesus as Lord and asked for forgiveness. 1 John 1:9 promises, "If we confess our sins, He is faithful and just to forgive us our sins and to cleanse us from all unrighteousness."

The enemy is crafty. He is subtle. He knows if he can get you focused on your past you will remain focused on your flaws and shortcomings. His goal is to keep you focused on your sin instead of focused on who you are IN CHRIST! But Jesus has REDEEMED YOU FROM THE CURSE! He has MADE YOU THE RIGHTEOUSNESS OF GOD IN HIM! YOU ARE FORGIVEN—JUSTIFIED—AND FREE IN JESUS!

If Satan can keep you stuck in sin consciousness you won't accomplish anything that Jesus came to free you to do. Romans 8:1-2, "[1]There is therefore now no condemnation to those who are in Christ Jesus, who do not walk according to the flesh, but according to the Spirit. [2]For the law of the Spirit of life in Christ Jesus has made me free from the law of sin and death."

In other words, YOU have been given diplomatic immunity from your past, present, and future sin, if you are a born-again Believer. Jesus has paid the price to RELEASE YOU FROM THE BONDAGE OF SIN and to MAKE YOU FREE! Does this give you the right to go out and willfully sin all you want—NO! But when you do sin, repent and then receive the grace that has been made available to you in Christ. Get back out there and finish doing what God has called you to do—by making His name famous!

Tell others about the grace and goodness you have received In Him. Let them know you're not perfect, but your Savior Jesus IS! Tell them that because of Jesus' perfect substitutional sacrifice— God's anger, His wrath, has been turned from us and was placed on Jesus. Let them know that God isn't mad at them. Tell everyone that God is madly in love with them and wants them to come back home. He wants them to experience His freedom, grace, love, Blessing, peace, and joy In Jesus. Hallelujah, I am so thankful for God's GRACE!

Daily Declaration

I receive God's grace today! I have been redeemed from the curse of sin and restored back to right standing in Jesus! Jesus has paid the price for my past, present, and future sins and I will no longer allow guilt and shame to keep me from receiving God's never ending love for me. Lord Jesus, I believe what 1 Corinthians 1:27-31 (MSG) tells me who I was before I received You as my Lord, and who I became after I received Your unmerited grace and favor. Paul writes, "Take a good look, friends, at who you were when you got called into this life. I don't see many of "the brightest and the best" among you, not many influential, not many from high-society families. Isn't it obvious that God deliberately chose men and women that the culture overlooks and exploits and abuses, chose these "nobodies" to expose the hollow pretensions of the "somebodies"? That makes it quite clear that none of you can get by with blowing your own horn before God. Everything that we have— right thinking and right living, a clean slate and a fresh start—comes from God by way of Jesus Christ. That's why we have the saying, "If you're going to blow a horn, blow a trumpet for God." Lord Jesus, thank You for making me a somebody in You. Heavenly Father, I receive all of Your grace for me today, in Jesus' mighty name, Amen.

Day 25
Frustration: The Fear That Your Efforts Are Getting You Nowhere

"Hope deferred makes the heart sick, but when the desire comes, it is a tree of life."

Proverbs 13:12 (NKJV)

Frustration is a tactic that the enemy uses to try to steal our joy, kill our dreams, and destroy our faith in God. He knows that if he can somehow get us to believe that God is uninterested in our affairs or that He is unwilling to intervene on our behalf, that we will assume He doesn't love us. The Devil knows that if we ever come to the place where we believe that it's no use even trying to live by faith— he has won the battle for our lives!

1 John 5:4 (AMP) tells us, "For whatever [whoever] is born of God is victorious over the world; and this is the victory that conquers the world, even our faith." If Satan can convince us to quit using our faith, he can render us impotent against his attacks. We are fighting a spiritual war and battling against unseen foes who are literally Hell bent on taking us out any way they can. That is why the Apostle Paul warned us to suit up in our spiritual armor every day.

Ephesians 6:11-18 (AMP) says, "[11] Put on God's whole armor [the armor of a heavy-armed soldier which God supplies], that you may be able successfully to stand up against [all] the strategies and the deceits of the devil. [12] For we are not wrestling with flesh and blood [contending only with physical opponents], but against the despotisms, against the powers, against [the master spirits who are] the world rulers of this present darkness, against the spirit forces of wickedness in the   heavenly (supernatural) sphere. [13] Therefore put on God's complete armor, that you may be able to resist and stand your ground on the evil day [of danger], and, having done all [the crisis demands], to stand [firmly in your place]. [14] Stand therefore [hold your ground], having tightened the belt of truth around your loins and having put on the breastplate of integrity and of moral rectitude and right standing with God, [15] And having shod your feet in preparation [to face the enemy with the firm-footed stability, the promptness, and the readiness produced by the good news] of the Gospel of peace. [16] Lift up over all the [covering] shield of saving faith, upon which you can quench all the flaming missiles of the wicked [one]. [17] And take the helmet of salvation and the sword that the Spirit wields, which is the Word of God. [18] Pray at all times (on every occasion, in every season) in the Spirit, with all [manner of] prayer and entreaty. To that end keep alert and watch with strong purpose and perseverance, interceding in behalf of all the saints (God's consecrated people)."

Paul spent quite a bit of time in Roman prisons and he became familiar with their armor. During this era of history, the Roman army was the most powerful military force in all the earth. Paul instructed us to put on the whole armor of God. Not just a few pieces here and there—but the FULL ARMOR. Otherwise we would leave some of our vital organs exposed and vulnerable to the enemy's attack. Let's take a moment to discuss our spiritual armor and what it is used for.

We have got to first understand that nothing is off limits in war. In Ephesians 6:11 Paul tells us why we need armor in the first place, "So that you may be able successfully to stand up against [all] the strategies and deceits of the devil." The enemy doesn't play fair! He will lie through his teeth and then stab you in the back when you are least expecting it—even after he's called a truce with you. The Bible calls him the Father of lies and says there is NO TRUTH in him. (See John 8:44).

The first piece of armor that Paul tells us to put on is the belt of truth. We've got to have a compass that always directs us to the truth, and that is exactly what the Word of God does. The reason that Paul used a belt as the symbol for truth is because the Roman soldiers wore a lot of gear that they would harness and tether together with their belts. Their belts were a crucial part of their entire list of gear because not only did it hold everything together, but other vital pieces of armor rested on their belt—including their swords. For the Christian, it is the Truth of the Word of God that holds every part of our lives together when we are in spiritual warfare and when we are enjoying times of peace. The Word of God is our standard for every decision in life! The Bible is our moral and spiritual compass which directs us into God's truth and away from Satan's deception.

The second piece of armor that Paul tells us to put on is the Breastplate of Righteousness. Just like the enemy wants to frustrate our efforts and turn us away from God by telling us lies about God and lies about ourselves, his most common objective is to get us to doubt God's love for us by pointing out our flaws and our past sins. He wants us to believe that we do not qualify or deserve God's Blessing. That's where the Breastplate of Righteousness comes in handy. The Breastplate of Righteousness covers all of our vital organs including our heart. Wearing it, reminds us that we are not made righteous because of our own works, but that we have been MADE THE RIGHTEOUSNESS OF GOD IN CHRIST, because of what Jesus did on the cross and because we have put our faith in Him as our Lord and Savior. In other words our righteousness is not earned or deserved but it is freely given by God because of His immeasurable love and grace to us.

2 Corinthians 5:21 (KJV) tells us, "For He [Our Heavenly Father] hath made him [Jesus] to be sin for us, who knew no sin; *that we might be made the righteousness of God in him.*" (Emphasis Added).

Next, Paul tells us to "shod" our feet with the Gospel of Peace. I believe this peace is two-fold: first, we must understand that it is only through believing God's Word—His precious promises in the Bible that we can have confidence and inner peace in this world.

Jesus said in John 14:1 and 27, "Let not your heart be troubled; you believe in God, believe also in Me… Peace I leave with you, My peace I give to you; not as the world gives do I give to you. Let not your heart be troubled, neither let it be afraid."

In Philippians 4:6-7 we read, "[6] Be anxious for nothing, but in everything by prayer and supplication, with thanksgiving, let your requests be made known to God; [7] *and the peace of God*, which surpasses all understanding, *will guard your hearts and minds through Christ Jesus*." (Emphasis Added).

It is only when we understand God's will for our lives, that we can enjoy true peace, even during our periods of intense trials and tribulations.

Secondly, the peace that Paul was instructing us to put on is the understanding that God wants us to experience wholeness, peace, and salvation in every facet of our lives. The word for peace in Hebrew is *Shalom* and the word for peace in Greek is *Eirene*. Each of these words means safety, security, protection, soundness, wholeness, perfect health, prosperity, lacking nothing, and harmony in life.

It is this kind of peace that we receive from God which gives us sure footing so that we can stand firm, even when we are in the midst of intense spiritual battles and fighting for our lives.

When the doctor tells us that we have an incurable disease, it is the peace that we receive from the promises in God's Word which assure us that healing belongs to us IN CHRIST! It is this confidence in the promises of God that give us the strength to persevere in our victory over sickness and death!

Strength and the determination to defeat our enemy come when we read Scriptures like Isaiah 26:3 which promises, "You [oh God] will keep him in perfect peace, whose mind is stayed on You, because he trusts in You." Or when we read Scriptures like Psalm 107:20 which says, "He sent His word and healed them, and delivered them from [All] their destructions."

Next, Paul tells us to take the Shield of faith to quench the fiery darts of the enemy. The shield that the Romans used was approximately four feet in height and about two and a half feet wide. When an opposing army would try to attack from afar by raining down arrows upon them, the Roman soldiers would huddle together locking their shields creating an impenetrable tortoise shell of sorts. This amazing protective maneuver would keep their enemies from harming then during an attack. If you have seen movies such as *The Lord of the Rings* or *300* you know exactly what I am talking about.

This idea of locking our shields together with other soldiers reminds me of Matthew 18:18-20 (AMP) which says, "[18] Truly I tell you, whatever you forbid and declare to be improper and unlawful on earth must be what is already forbidden in heaven, and whatever you permit and declare proper and lawful on earth must be what is already permitted in heaven. [19] *Again I tell you, if two of you on earth agree (harmonize together, make a symphony together)* about whatever [anything and everything] they may ask, it will come to pass and be done for them by My Father in heaven. [20] *For wherever two or three are gathered (drawn together as My followers) in (into) My name, there I AM in the midst of them.*" (Emphasis Added).

Paul describes the protective armor which covers our heads and our minds, as the Helmet of Salvation. The greatest battlefield in which the Devil opposes us is the battlefield of the mind. The enemy continually tries to bombard our minds with negative thoughts, doubts, fears, and reminders of our past sins. He is always trying to shake our confidence in the complete salvation which Jesus has provided for us. When you received Jesus as your Lord and Savior,

He forgave you of every sin you have ever committed. Those sins have been lost in the sea of forgetfulness and will never again be remembered by God. The problem however, is that even though God has forgotten them, the Devil is an expert at helping us to remember them. He tries to   condemn us of things God has already forgiven.

If you struggle with guilt and shame for past sins allow Romans 8:1-2 to become your life verses. "There is therefore now no condemnation to those who are in Christ Jesus, who do not walk according to the flesh, but according to the Spirit. [2] *For the law of the Spirit of life in Christ Jesus has made me free from the law of sin and death.*" (Emphasis Added). 1 John 1:9 is another great verse which helps us to remember God's faithfulness when we humble ourselves before Him. "If we confess our sins, He is faithful and just to forgive us our sins and to cleanse us from all unrighteousness."

Your salvation is secure in Jesus. The lies of the devil are just that—lies, meant to frustrate and convince you that you aren't worthy of God's amazing love, and to get you off your mission. But don't fall for them—put on the full armor of God.

Finally, Paul tells us to take the Sword of the Spirit which is the Word of God, praying at all times in the Spirit. The Roman sword was about two feet in length and had a sharp edge on each side. Any way the soldier thrust his sword, it was sure to cut and do damage.

Our sword is the Word of God—the Bible. Hebrews 4:12 tells us, "For the word of God is living and powerful, and sharper than any two-edged sword, piercing even to the division of soul and spirit, and of joints and marrow, and is a discerner of the thoughts and intents of the heart."

The Word of God will defeat the enemy every time, and cut him to shreds. Jesus defeated Satan when he tried to tempt Jesus in the wilderness. Each time the enemy tried to get Jesus to do something Jesus would respond by saying—"IT IS WRITTEN" (See Matthew 4:4-7).

The Word of God in your mouth is just as powerful as it is, in God's mouth. That is why prayer is so foundational in the Believer's life. When we pray in our native tongue or when we pray in the spirit, we deliver fatal blows to the kingdom of darkness. Moreover, when the enemy comes at us trying to attack God's character or our sure foundation IN JESUS—we can send him packing by using the Word of God as the basis for our rebuttal to all of his attacks. The Word, The Name of JESUS, and HIS BLOOD which was shed as the payment for our sins—ALWAYS PREVAILS over the lies of the enemy!

That is why Paul instructed us to pray at all times. When we pray in the spirit, we release prayers that are often bigger than our mortal mind can fathom. They are Holy Ghost inspired prayers that take out entire legions of devils and send them running for cover.

Frustration and fear is always the outcome of listening to the lies of the Devil. Make a promise to yourself from this moment forward not to waste your time listening to him. Instead, stay plugged into the Word and feed your faith!

When you have the opportunity to become discouraged because you aren't yet seeing the results you have been praying for—get into the Word and build yourself up on your most holy faith by praying in the Spirit! *The Devil is looking to see if he can find a chink in your armor*! He is looking for a way to get at your spirit to start speaking his lies. Don't ever leave the house without putting on the FULL ARMOR OF GOD. If you do you'll risk losing the battle he'll unleash upon you.

An interesting thing I have learned is that Satan always tries to attack me the hardest right before my breakthrough is manifested. He does his best to convince me that things will always remain the way they are, that they'll never get any better, or that I should just throw in the towel and give up.

But 2 Corinthians 5:7 instructs us to walk by faith and not by sight. We are to believe the Word of God over our present circumstances. When everything looks hopeless, it just means that it's time to put our praise and thanksgiving into high gear. It means that we will see our victory at any moment *if we don't give up!* The Devil always uses frustration to try to convince us that our efforts are leading us nowhere—but remember—he's a liar! Instead of throwing in your towel, check your armor, make sure you are wearing it all and that there are no vital organs exposed. Then continue fighting the Good fight of faith knowing that the Battle is the Lord's but the Victory is YOURS! Keep wielding your sword, keep speaking the Word, and tell frustration to go jump in the lake— the Lake of Fire! Amen!

Daily Declaration

I declare that no weapon formed against me shall prosper in the name of Jesus! I have put on the FULL ARMOR of God which is impenetrable by any of Satan's forces. My faith is established on the Word of God which is the will of God for my life. The Bible tells me that I have overcome Satan through the BLOOD of Jesus and the WORD of God which I speak continually. (See Revelation 12:11) 1 John 4:4 says of me, "You are of God, little children, and have overcome them, because He who is in you is greater than he who is in the world." Jesus is IN ME and He leads me in constant VICTORY over Satan and his imps. 2 Corinthians 2:14 promises, "Now thanks be to God who always leads us in triumph in Christ…" I am shouting my victory right now. I AM BLESSED! I AM HIGHLY FAVORED of God! I AM VICTORIOUS IN JESUS! Devil, I serve you an eviction notice and I declare—IT IS WRITTEN, "Submit to God. Resist the devil and he will flee from you." I have submitted to God. I have resisted you devil, so all that is left is for you to tuck your tail and RUN—IN THE NAME OF JESUS! Thank You Father for Your Word, for Your Son Jesus, and for my impenetrable Armor! I love You Lord, and I pray all of this in the mighty name of Jesus, Amen!

Day 26
Is It A Promotion Or Just A Distraction?

"For a day in Your courts is better than a thousand [anywhere else]; I would rather be a doorkeeper and stand at the threshold in the house of my God than to dwell [at ease] in the tents of wickedness."

Psalm 84:10 (AMP)

Years ago when I was preparing to leave the pharmaceutical company I was working for, and getting ready to move my family to Tulsa, Oklahoma so that I could attend Oral Robert's University, an "incredible opportunity" was mysteriously offered to me. A well-known pharmaceutical company contacted me and offered me double my salary to stay in California and go to work for them. They were offering double the money for managing a much smaller territory than I had been managing. They promised bonuses and benefits that were almost too good to be true. I must admit, I was half tempted to take the job and bypass the plan I knew God had for my life. But deep inside my spirit something, or should I say SOMEONE said, "Mike, this is just a distraction to lure you away from My Best. It is an attempt to draw you away from your destiny."

Satan is a student of people. He understands the fallen Human Condition caused by sin and he uses that knowledge to his advantage. He will dangle those golden carrots, those "things" that motivate and tempt us—things that aren't necessarily bad in themselves—in order to steer us away from God's BEST for our lives. Satan wants to keep us from reaching our full potential and from becoming a greater threat to his kingdom. These "things" are often packaged as: money, people we love, or jobs and other opportunities, which will tempt or distract us away from OUR FIRST LOVE—God.

Jesus said it this way in Revelation 2:3-4 (AMP), "[3] I know you are enduring patiently and are bearing up for My name's sake, and you have not fainted or become exhausted or grown weary. [4] But I have this [one charge to make] against you: that you have left (abandoned) the love that you had at first [you have deserted Me, your first love]."

Have you allowed the enemy to distract you away from the things of God? Have you put your pursuit of obtaining "the Good Life" above your call to live a devoted life to Him?

In Matthew 6:32-33 (AMP) Jesus tells us that our Heavenly Father understands every detail concerning our needs and desires. Jesus warns not to fall into Satan's trap. He warns us not to be led astray through the Devil's sly deception—or by taking the "easy way out." "[32] For the Gentiles (heathen) wish for and crave and diligently seek all these things, and your heavenly Father knows well that you need them all. [33] But seek (aim at and strive after) first of all His kingdom and His righteousness (His way of doing and being right), and then all these things taken together will be given you besides."

In Hebrews 4:15 we learn that Jesus was in all points tempted as we are. He faced the same opportunities to chase after things instead of chasing after God. Yet, He overcame that temptation and so will we if we put Him and His plan for our lives above our personal gain. I'm not suggesting that we take a vow of poverty. No! But I am suggesting that we understand that when we put God first, true prosperity is the outcome—spiritual prosperity, emotional prosperity, mental prosperity, physical prosperity, and even financial prosperity.

One of the things that completely shocked me when I got to ORU was something that my advisor said during our first meeting. He was an elderly gentleman who had been in the ministry for many years. He had not only been pastoring a large "Word Church" for decades, but this man had also been teaching at Oral Robert's University for thirty years. As I listened to him speak, I wondered how he could claim to believe the Bible. His heart, his faith, his real beliefs about God and His promises, didn't (in my personal opinion) fit with what he actually professed to believe.

What I am saying is his title and his position as a leading authority in a Charismatic, Word of Faith university should predispose him to believe that, "Nothing is impossible for the person who believes God and acts on His Word." (See Mark 9:23).

After introducing himself and explaining his role as my advisor, he asked me to share a little about my background. He began asking questions about my professional life prior to moving to Tulsa. When I answered him about my career in the pharmaceutical industry, he said something that made my stomach turn. "You'll never make that kind of money in ministry!"

I looked at him a little rattled, but then calmly told him that I hadn't gotten into "the ministry" for the money. I explained that I respected his personal opinion, but that I had to disagree with what he was saying because Jesus promised in Mark 10:29-30, "Assuredly, I say to you, *there is no one who has left* house or brothers or sisters or father or mother or wife or children or lands, for My sake and the gospel's, [30] *who shall not receive a hundredfold now in this time*—houses and brothers and sisters and mothers and children and lands, with persecutions—*and in the age to come, eternal life*." [Emphasis Added].

I told him I had sown my career in order to fulfill God's call on my life. I told him I believed that God would honor my faith and I would not need to worry about money. After all, didn't Philippians 4:19 promise us that God would meet **ALL** of our needs according to HIS RICHES in glory, through CHIRST JESUS?

Being bold to share my faith with this man didn't win me any popularity points, but it sure made me feel better. He immediately shuffled papers together, realizing that he had overstepped his boundaries and said, "Yes, well ok, good," and that was the end of our first conversation.

I realized then and there that the enemy will use people who "look the part," to try to sway and deter us in our faith. Satan is the master of "legalistic and religious thinking." He wants our focus to be on meeting our own needs instead of allowing God to be our source. He wants us to believe that if we truly go after God and work for Him that we are sentencing ourselves to a sub-par life. The devil wants to get our focus off of what really matters—the eternal lives of everyone around us—and to get us to become self-centered and afraid.

He will use people who are supposed to know better, people who are supposed to help guide us in our journey of faith, to point us in the wrong direction, away from God's Master plan for our lives.

In a real sense this man was sharing a truth from his personal experience. I sincerely believe that he was trying to help me and to share what he thought would keep me from making a horrible mistake. He was telling me that if I was smart, I'd go back to the pharmaceutical job I had just left. He believed that though it was "noble" to work in ministry—that doing so was akin to taking a vow of poverty.

Jesus spoke about people like this in Matthew 15:6-9. He rebuked this type of bogus faith when He said, "You have made the commandment of God of no effect by your tradition. [7]Hypocrites! Well did Isaiah prophesy about you, saying: [8]'These people draw near to Me with their mouth, and honor Me with their lips, but their heart is far from Me. [9] And in vain they worship Me, teaching as doctrines the commandments of men.'"

This man's personal belief system was that money was more important than being obedient to the call of God. His tradition based on his personal experience taught him that trusting God would lead him to Heaven, but that it had also doomed him to living a life filled with lack and want.

Though we all face trials in life, Psalm 34:10 promises us, "The young lions lack and suffer hunger; but *those who seek the LORD shall not lack any good thing.*" [Emphasis Added]

Psalm 37:4 instructs us to, "Delight yourself also in the LORD, and *He shall give you the desires of your heart.*" [Emphasis Added].

And Isaiah 1:19 promises, "The willing and obedient, shall eat the good of the land."

Don't be swindled out of your inheritance! Don't be duped out of your destiny! And don't be deceived by things that" look like" they may be a promotion, when in reality they are a distraction! The Devil is always looking for ways to take you out of the presence and plan of God. He may try to convince you that God is trying to give you a promotion in your job, but when that so called "promotion" keeps you out of church on Sundays by demanding that you work those days—IT'S A DISTRACTION! When your "promotion" makes you compromise your values or takes you away from the things that really matter, like family—then it's not really a promotion—IT'S A DISTRACTION!

God's Promotions will ALWAYS line up with the His Word. They will ALWAYS cause you to use your faith. And they will ALWAYS draw you closer to Him and to the things that truly matter in life. Don't settle for the Devils' substitutes which always come at a price. Instead, believe your way into the REAL THING!

Psalm 84:10 tells us, One day in the courts of God is better than a thousand days anywhere else. Make God and His Kingdom your first and highest priority! You will not only thrive in God's courts but you will also enjoy true promotion in this life and in the one to come.

You're not sacrificing your dreams or desires by passing up the bogus deal that Satan has disguised as your divine "promotion." When you say, "NO!" to those tempting distractions, you are sowing a seed of your faith that will blossom into God's VERY BEST. True Promotion only comes from God. His kind of promotion will require you to use your faith, but it will also lead you to PEACE of mind, PEACE in your spirit, and PEACE in your relationship with Him and others. Go for the real deal! I declare that Promotion is coming your way in Jesus' Name! Amen!

Daily Declaration

I declare that I am enjoying real promotion and I rebuke Satan and all of the distractions that he would use to try to move me out of the PERFECT WILL OF GOD. Psalm 75:6-7 (KJV) declares, "[6] For **PROMOTION** cometh neither from the east, nor from the west, nor from the south. [7] But God is the judge: he putteth down one, and setteth up another." [Emphasis Added]. God has BLESSED me! I have humbled myself under His authority and He has exalted me through Jesus! 1 Peter 5:6 (MSG) promises, "So be content with who you are, and don't put on airs. God's strong hand is on you; he'll promote you at the right time." Heavenly Father, I thank You for your grace and for Your supernatural favor on my life! I thank You that no matter what happens You always have my best interest at heart. Father, I am determined to seek You and Your will first. You are my priority and my first and foremost love! Thank You for meeting my needs and my desires! Your thoughts are higher than my thoughts and Your ways are higher than my ways. (See Isaiah 55:8-9). Even though it may look as if I am making the wrong decision by taking a job that pays less money than another one, but it allows me to focus on the things that truly matter, I will trust You to lead me into Real Victory. You are my Source not my job! You are my God and I want to live a life that is pleasing to You! I pray these things in Jesus' mighty name, Amen.

Day 27
Shout…You Prosperity Magnet You!

"Let them shout for joy and be glad, who favor my righteous cause; and let them say continually, "Let the LORD be magnified, Who has pleasure in the prosperity of His servant."

Psalm 35:27 (NKJV)

A lot of people want to argue about prosperity and whether or not it is part of the "salvation" Jesus made available through His death on the Cross. Some have an axe to grind with those of us who teach that **it IS God's will for us to be PROSPEROUS—*SPIRITUALLY, SOULISHLY*** (in our mind, will, and emotions), ***BODILY*** (in our health and well-being), and yes, even ***FINANCIALLY!***

They often say something like, "Oh, you're just one of those prosperity preachers." Well I'll tell you what, teaching people how to overcome and how they can live in victory because of what Jesus made available through the cross, is ***ALWAYS*** better than lying to them and convincing them that God wants them broke, sick, defeated, and abused by the devil. The TRUTH ***ALWAYS*** triumphs over lies! And God's will for ***ALL*** of His people is WHOLENESS IN EVERY FACET OF LIFE!

If you were to study out this Scripture from the Hebrew, the word translated prosperity is the Hebrew word *Shalom*. The definition of *Shalom* is peace, wholeness, welfare, safety, to be untroubled, fulfilled, content, **PROSPEROUS**, to be FREE FROM OPPRESSION and FEAR, to be DELIVERED from ALL HARM, and to live in complete HARMONY WITH GOD IN WHICH ALL OF YOUR NEEDS ARE MET IN AND THROUGH HIM!

Shalom is the opposite of EVERYTHING that is connected to the curse! Read Deuteronomy 28. Lack, sickness, poverty, bad relationships, not enough, the absence of rest, worry, anxiety, stress, defeat, abuse, hardship, those are all part of the Curse.

In Galatians 3:13-14 we read, "[13] Christ has redeemed us from the curse of the law, having become a curse for us (for it is written, "Cursed is everyone who hangs on a tree"), [14] that the blessing of Abraham might come upon the Gentiles in Christ Jesus, that we might receive the promise of the Spirit through faith." The question then becomes, what is the BLESSING of Abraham? The answer to that question is found in the first fourteen verses of Deuteronomy 28.

"[1] If you fully obey the LORD your God and carefully keep all his commands that I am giving you today, the LORD your God will set you high above all the nations of the world. [2] You will experience all these blessings if you obey the LORD your God: [3] Your towns and your fields will be blessed. [4] Your children and your crops will be blessed. The offspring of your herds and flocks will be blessed. [5] Your fruit baskets and breadboards will be blessed. [6] Wherever you go and whatever you do, you will be blessed. [7] "The LORD will conquer your enemies when they attack you. They will attack you from one direction, but they will scatter from you in seven! [8] "The LORD will guarantee a blessing on everything you do and will fill your storehouses with grain. The LORD your God will bless you in the land he is giving you. [9] "If you obey the commands of the LORD your God and walk in his ways, the LORD will establish you as his holy people as he swore he would do. [10] Then all the nations of the world will see that you are a people claimed by the LORD, and they will stand in awe of you. [11] *"**The LORD will give you prosperity** in the land he swore to your ancestors to give you, blessing you with many children, numerous livestock, and abundant crops.* [12] The LORD will send rain at the proper time from his rich treasury in the heavens *and will bless all the work you do*. You will lend to many nations, but you will never need to borrow from them. [13] If you listen to these commands of the LORD your God that I am giving you today, and if you carefully obey them, *the LORD will make you the head and not the tail, and you will always be on top and never at the bottom.* [14] You must not turn away from any of the commands I am giving you today, nor follow after other gods and worship them." (Deuteronomy 28:1-14, NLT) [Emphasis Added].

Now go back to Galatians 3:29 which promises us, "And if you are Christ's, then you are Abraham's seed, and heirs according to the promise." NOW THAT IS GROUNDS FOR SHOUTING!!!

Because of what Jesus did on the cross, you and I not only have access to Heaven when we die, but we have access to all that the BLESSING offers us! We have access to WHOLENESS in our marriages, WHOLENESS in our bodies, WHOLENESS in our finances, WHOLENESS in our mind and spirit, and WHOLENESS in our relationships. Anything less than WHOLENESS is part of the Curse!

I don't know about you, but I want EVERYTHING that Jesus has made available to me! I want all of His goodness, all of His love, all of the BLESSING that he has willingly given to me. Moreover, I want to be able to share it with everyone I know. That is what God meant when He told Abraham that He BLESSED him so that he could be a Blessing to others.

God did the same with David in Psalm 23. David testified to the fact that his cup was running over, that he had more than enough, and that God's mercy and unmerited favor was following him all the days of his life. God wasn't wasting whatever it was He was pouring into David's cup, by allowing it to run over! He was creating more than enough so that David would have enough to meet his needs and still have more available to share with others! God wanted David and He also wants us to BE witnesses of His goodness! He wants us tell everyone that we come in contact with just how good it is to serve an amazing God who takes pleasure in prosperity of His people! Lift up your voice...IT'S TIME TO SHOUT letting everyone know that GOD IS GOOD, that He takes pleasure in the PROSPERITY of His people, and that we are magnets to His BLESSING!!!

Daily Declaration

I declare that I am a prosperity magnet! I am a magnet to the BLESSING of God in Jesus! God has commanded His BLESSING on me. (See Deuteronomy 28:8). And Proverbs 10:22 (AMP) says, "The blessing of the Lord—it makes [truly] rich, and He adds no sorrow with it [neither does toiling increase it]." I will not allow the Devil, Man's traditions, or anything else, to cheat me out of what God has willfully given to me. As part of the Body of Christ it is my responsibility to be a witness of God's goodness in the earth and to help send the message of the Gospel by using some of the resources He has Blessed me with. Poverty, Lack, and insufficiency are all part of the Curse. Jesus has redeemed me from the Curse by becoming the Curse for me! I AM Redeemed! I AM Blessed! And I AM Prosperous in EVERY sense of the word! No one has to be Jealous of me—they can join in and LIVE BLESSED by receiving Jesus as Lord! God is not limited or lacking in any way. My God is a More Than Enough God! He is *El Shaddai*, the Almighty God who is whatever we need Him to be—Savior, Lord, Protector, redeemer, Provider, etc. Father, thank You for being my God! I love You and thank You for Your Son Jesus! I pray and declare all of these things over my life in the strong name of Jesus. The Name which is above the names of poverty, lack, and not enough! I pray these things in Jesus name, Amen.

Day 28
You Have Access To Riches In Jesus

"For you know the grace of our Lord Jesus Christ, that though He was rich, yet for your sakes He became poor, that you through His poverty might become rich."

2 Corinthians 8:9 (NKJV)

D o you believe this promise from the Bible? Do you believe in God's goodness, His grace, and that it is His will for you to prosper? Or, do you pick and choose which things you will believe from the Bible and which things you won't? God made the only qualification for your receiving His promises as YOUR belief in Jesus as YOUR Lord and YOUR faith in His Word!

Are you one of those people who says, "Well what Paul meant when he was teaching this passage was that Jesus became "spiritually poor" that you might become "spiritually rich"? That is a lie of the devil! A "spiritually poor" person could not raise Lazarus from the dead! A "spiritually poor" person couldn't heal the blind or the lame, the deaf or the mute people who came to Him for their healing! A "spiritually poor" person couldn't feed 5000 people with a two piece fish dinner and a couple of biscuits! Moreover, a "spiritually poor" Jesus couldn't save YOU and ME from the Hell that we deserve because of our sin! Jesus was not SPIRITUALLY POOR!

No! Jesus left the extravagance of Heaven to make us rich in every area of our lives—spirit, soul, and body. Don't discount what Jesus did to restore you back into right standing with the Father. Don't overlook what he did where relationships with others are concerned. Don't disregard what he did so that we could be healed and rich in our bodies. Don't throw out what Jesus did to free us from the effects of the Curse, which include freeing us from poverty, lack, and not enough! Jesus is our Deliverer! He's our Redeemer! And He's our Savior! He has redeemed us from every symptom of the Curse and brought us back into Right Standing with God! We don't lack anything now that we are IN JESUS! We have become heirs of God and Joint-heirs with Christ—Hallelujah! (See Romans 8:16-17).

Don't allow some ignorant person to cheat you out of what rightfully belongs to you in Christ Jesus. I don't care if they claim to be a Christian or even a minister of the Gospel! Stick with the Word of God and you will never go wrong. The Word *ALWAYS* works! Jesus came and died so that you could be BLESSED! Blessed in your spirit, Blessed in your soul, Blessed in your body, and Blessed in your material needs. Is your employment included in that blessing? Yes, it is! You are a Child of the Most High God, and He has given you the power to get wealth (See Deuteronomy 8:18). Your Blessing, Your wealth is a covenant thing with Him! He has promised to care for and Bless you by making you a Blessing to others!

Speak victory to your workplace today. Speak victory to your check book, your bank accounts, your food pantry. Tell everything and everyone that you are in line for promotion, increase, and the favor of God. Speak to that job you're believing God for—call it in to you with your faith! Speak Blessing over your family, over your pets, and over your health. Then give God the glory for being your Source, for being your Provider, and trust Him to manifest the desires of your heart. Jesus became poor so that you would be made rich and Blessed in Him! He is your access to the Blessing of God! There is no recession in Heaven—Jesus isn't worried about having to sell the Pearly Gates to meet your needs like He promised to—So don't take part in any recession down here either! Jesus Is Lord—and He is Rich in the Blessing of God and so are You—IN HIM!

Daily Declaration

I declare that I have everything that I need in Jesus. Colossians 2:10 tells me that I am complete IN HIM. Father I thank You that you have made me rich and have delivered me from lack of every kind through Jesus. Jesus became poor so that I would be made RICH! I Am Rich, I AM Wealthy, I AM Healthy, I AM Whole, I AM Blessed, and I AM Victorious over sin, sickness, death, and the Curse! I declare in the name of Jesus that I AM a money magnet. God's Supernatural Favor and Anointing surround me like a shield. Angels go before me and behind me clear away all of the obstacles that would try to hinder me from reaching my destiny and my destination! I Am an Overcomer in Jesus! I speak to every mountain that tries to stand in my way and I command it to move and to be cast in the sea. (See Mark 11:23-24). In the name of Jesus, mountain of debt, mountain of lack, mountain of sickness, and every other hindering mountain, I bind you in Jesus' name. I command you to cease and desist in your attacks against me! I render you harmless and ineffective against me in the name of Jesus! And I command you to be cast into the sea. Ministering spirits go now and bring in my harvest. I Am a sower! I Am a tither, and God has promised to open up the windows of Heaven and to pour out a Blessing that is too much for me to receive it all in. (See Malachi 3:10). Jesus has made me rich and I receive all that He has provided for me now! I pray all of these things in Jesus' name, Amen.

Day 29
Believing Leads To Seeing…Not The Reverse

"Then Jesus said to the centurion, "Go your way; and as you have believed, so let it be done for you." And his servant was healed that same hour."

Matthew 8:13 (NKJV)

What do you believe? I understand that this is a fairly vague question, but it is a very important one. What do you believe about yourself? What do you believe about those around you? Most importantly, what do you believe about God and His Word?

What you believe determines your attitude. Your belief determines how you act, what you talk about, and ultimately where you will end-up in life. If you believe that something is too hard, you will limit yourself and never accomplish that task. If you view something as being too expensive, you will never have the faith to ever receive it and enjoy it. Your subconscious mind will stop you from receiving those things that you do not have the faith to believe you can have—your lack of faith will disqualify you from ever having the ability to receive it.

If you believe that you're not smart enough, not pretty enough, not worthy…, these are all beliefs that limit your ability to receive from God. Psychologists call it Self-fulfilling Prophecy, but God calls it Fear and Doubt!

In order to receive the promises of God and the desires of your heart, you must begin to BELIEVE. Believe that you are who God says you are! Believe that you can have what He says you can have. And believe that you can do what He says you can do.

The Bible promises that we can do all things in Christ who strengthens us (SEE Philippians 4:13). The most important thing that we must believe and receive is the love of God for us. If we do not believe that God loves us, then we will never have the faith that He will ever do anything to Bless our lives. Let me tell you something— Our Heavenly Father has already done EVERYTHING we could ever need Him to do for us! That may sound crazy to you—but it's true! God sent Jesus as the perfect substitution for our sin. Jesus died the death that we should have died. He was buried and went to Hell. He overcame Hell, defeated Satan, and was raised-up by the Father to sit at His right-hand.

As a result we have total access to everything God owns. He has not only provided an eternal destination for us in Heaven, but He has also provided—Healing, Prosperity, Healthy Emotions, Healthy Relationships, and Deliverance from every demonic stronghold we will ever face.

Our Heavenly Father loves us as much as He loves Jesus. (SEE John 17:23). In fact some might say that Our Heavenly Father loves us even more, because He was willing to sacrifice Jesus on the Cross in order to receive us back into right relationship with Him.

The minute that you are able to believe, is the minute that miracles will begin to happen for you! Start believing today, by reading your Bible and by personalizing the promises that you find, as belonging to you. The entire purpose of making the Bible available to us was so God could let us know just how much He loves us and all that He has made available in Jesus. READ! MEDITATE! BELIEVE! And SPEAK THE WORD! When you do, you will WITNESS just how God's promise will come to pass in your life. Some people mistakenly say that seeing is believing—but that's just not true. There is no need to believe for something that you can already see. In reality, Believing leads to seeing—because faith is the substance of things hoped for, the evidence of things NOT SEEN! (Hebrews 11:1). Your faith in God will bring the invisible things you cannot see—into being things that are real and visible. When you believe God, your faith changes your circumstances, and like the centurion experienced, in that same hour...you could receive the reward of your faith...ONLY BELIEVE!

Daily Declaration

I declare that I am not moved but what I see or what I do not see. I am only moved by the promises of God! Lord Jesus, Your Word explains that faith has a voice. Faith speaks and mountains move. In fact, 2 Corinthians 4:13, 18 say, "And since we have the same spirit of faith, according to what is written, "I believed and therefore I spoke," we also believe and therefore speak…while we do not look at the things which are seen, but at the things which are not seen. For the things which are seen are temporary, but the things which are not seen are eternal." In other words, ___**NOTHING**___ is too hard for God or for a Believer who has the audacity to believe and speak God's promises, claiming them, based on the finished work of Jesus on the Cross! Thank You lord I Believe and I Receive all of Your promises! I call myself Blessed, Healed, Whole, Fully-Supplied, and Lacking Nothing in Jesus' Name! I Believe Your Word Lord; it opens up my life to Your Blessing! Thank You for Your faithfulness. I pray all of these things in Jesus' mighty name, Amen.

Day 30
The Enemy Wants To Convince
You That You're Helpless

"[17] But no weapon that is formed against you shall prosper, and
every tongue that shall rise against you in judgment you shall show
to be in the wrong. This [peace, righteousness, security, triumph over
opposition] is the heritage of the servants of the Lord [those in whom
the ideal Servant of the Lord is reproduced]; this is the righteousness
or the vindication which they obtain from Me [this is that which I
impart to them as their justification], says the Lord."

Isaiah 54:17 (AMP)

Did you know that you have been born into a family with a
heritage of victory? That you have been born into a family
with a never-ending heritage of triumph over the Devil?
Yes you have! This heritage is a spiritual heritage which has been
passed down from our spiritual forefathers and ratified in the
precious Blood of Jesus, and then passed directly to you. In fact, we
come from a long list of supernatural overcoming stock which
includes such faith heroes as Joshua, David, Paul, and JESUS!

You may not realize it, but as a Christian you have access to
immense power. The same power that created the universe and
raised Jesus from the dead! Ephesians 1:13-14 says, "In Him you
also trusted, after you heard the word of truth, the gospel of your
salvation; in whom also, having believed, you were SEALED with
the Holy Spirit of promise, [14] who is the guarantee of our
inheritance..." I know you don't have a bold "S" stamped on your
chest and a cape waiting in the wings, but you do have natural and
spiritual significance.

The Bible tells us that as a Believer and follower of Jesus you have been sealed and given a designating mark. A mark that represents purpose and opens up doors to success and God's unmerited favor! A mark which symbolizes to all of the demonic forces that YOU HAVE ALREADY WON EVERY BATTLE IN CHRIST!

But just like Superman's weakness was kryptonite, Believers have a weakness too: it's called sin. The good news is that Jesus has already dealt with that issue and defeated sin once and for all. You have in a sense been inoculated against sin and been give the ability to   overcome every attempt that sin makes against you, continuing on triumphantly in Jesus.

1 Corinthians 15:57 says, "But thanks be to God, who gives us the victory through our Lord Jesus Christ." 2 Corinthians 2:14 (MSG) tells us, "In the Messiah, in Christ, God leads us from place to place in one perpetual victory parade. Through us, he brings knowledge of Christ. Everywhere we go, people breathe in the exquisite fragrance. Because of Christ, we give off a sweet scent rising to God, which is recognized by those on the way of salvation—an aroma redolent with life."

The point is this, whenever you face challenges; whenever you're feeling a little beat up, whenever Satan is telling you that you won't win this battle, remind him that you've already been sealed. Remind him that you have already been marked for VICTORY over sin, sickness, and death! Remind him that no weapon formed against you will prosper—because Jesus has redeemed you from the Curse of the Law being made a Curse for you! Hallelujah! Remind him of the legacy of faith that runs through your spiritual veins. Tell him about your heritage of Victory, Triumph, and Overcoming Power in God! Remind him that God always gives you the victory in Jesus! And then give him a Bible lesson by telling him, "IT IS WRITTEN…" and list off all of the precious promises that God has made available to you IN JESUS!

If Satan has been telling you that you can't have something, quote him Psalm 37:4, 2 Corinthians 8:9, and Philippians 4:19. If he's been telling you that he is going to kill you with sickness and disease, remind him of Psalm 107:20; Isaiah 53:5; Matthew 8:17, and 1 Peter 2:24. Speak the Word to him and tell him to watch his tongue because you've just proved him wrong. Then tell him to SHUT UP AND TO FLEE FORM YOU!! You have a heritage of Victory, so don't let him convince you otherwise—he's a Liar and a defeated foe in Jesus!

Daily Declaration

I declare that IN JESUS I already have every Victory necessary to overcome Satan and his cohorts. God has delivered me from the power of darkness and translated me into the Kingdom of His Son, Jesus—The Son of His unending LOVE! (See Colossians 1:13). Not only have I been redeemed from the Curse, but I have been made a victor and not a victim! I am an Overcomer in Christ! In the name of Jesus, I bind you Satan! I bind every weapon that you have waged against me in Jesus' name! You are a liar and You no longer have any authority over my life! Jesus is my Lord! Jesus is my heritage— and in that heritage I have been made the RIGHTEOUS of God in Christ! In fact, 1 Corinthians 1:27-31 tells me, "²⁷ But God has chosen the foolish things of the world to put to shame the wise, and God has chosen the weak things of the world to put to shame the things which are mighty; ²⁸ and the base things of the world and the things which are despised God has chosen, and the things which are not, to bring to nothing the things that are, ²⁹ that no flesh should glory in His presence. ³⁰ *But of Him you are in Christ Jesus, who became for us wisdom from God—and righteousness and sanctification and redemption* ³¹ that, as it is written, "He who glories, let him glory in the LORD." [Emphasis Added]. I admit that I don't have anything to glory in over myself. I was foolish before meeting Jesus. I could have been considered the lowest of the low, but Jesus brought me out of that condition and loved me anyway. Just like the blind man whom Jesus healed in John 9:25, I can honestly say that I may not know much but, "One thing I know: that though I was blind, now I see." Thank You Jesus for rescuing me and for giving me a future in You! I receive all that you have for me and I pray all of these things in Jesus' mighty name, Amen!

FOLLOW US AS WE FOLLOW JESUS

On the web at:
www.michaelvidaurri.com

On Facebook at:
https://www.facebook.com/pages/Michael-Vidaurri-Ministries/361809073932887

On Twitter at:
https://twitter.com/mike_vidaurri

On LinkedIn at:
http://www.linkedin.com/pub/michael-vidaurri-d-min/66/36a/b6

Made in the USA
Coppell, TX
28 December 2021

70253572R00109